Statistics in Dialectology

Statistics in Dialectology

Lawrence M. Davis

The University of Alabama Press
TUSCALOOSA AND LONDON

∞

The paper on which this book is printed meets the minimum
requirements of American National Standard for Information
Science-Permanence of Paper for Printed Library Materials,
ANSI A39.48-1984.

Library of Congress Cataloging-in-Publication Data

Davis, Lawrence M.
    Statistics in dialectology / Lawrence M. Davis
        p.   cm.
    Includes index.
    Includes bibliographical references.
    ISBN 0-8173-0510-6 (pbk.) : $12.95
    1. Dialectology—Statistical methods.   I. Title.
P367.D38   1990   90-35856
417'.2'021—dc20   CIP

British Library Cataloguing-in-Publication Data available

For Dvorah (Guta) Rosenhouse and Sam J. Davis,
in loving memory

Contents

Tables and Figures

Tables

Figures

Preface

The purpose of this work is to outline the major statistical tests that may be of use to the dialectologist who analyzes quantitative linguistic data. The book assumes the reader's competence in mathematics to be at about the level of secondary school algebra. It assumes somewhat more knowledge of dialectology; that is, no attempt has been made here to prove that language varies or that language variation is patterned. This text also differs in many fundamental ways from introductory statistics textbooks. No attention has been given to the questions of set theory and probability theory which underlie statistical testing. In other words, I have ignored fundamental questions about why the various tests work; also, the different formulas are presented without regard to how they are derived mathematically. This text also differs from Anshen 1978, in that it is wider in scope, and from Butler 1985 and Hatch and Farhady 1982, in that it is more introductory in nature.

Given the introductory nature of this text, I have decided not to include a discussion of two important issues in the analysis of linguistic data: (1) the work on variable rules begun by Cedergren and Sankoff 1974, including their VARBRUL CP/M program, and (2) the work on multidimensional scaling by (for example) Cichocki 1988, Houck 1986, and Linn and Regal 1988.

All of the statistical operations in the following pages can be performed on a good scientific calculator. Some operations, however, such as two-way analysis of variance and the coefficient of correlation involving large samples, are extremely cumbersome, and good computer programs, such as SPSS, SPSS–X, SAS, or Minitab can save a lot of time. SAS and SPSS are also available for use on MS-DOS personal computers, and Statview SE+ is great with Macintosh SE's (or larger). My own calculator computes regression lines and correlation coefficients, not to mention squares and square roots, but I have found the computer to be indispensable. After all, in addition to making all those tedious computations, it also stores the data, rather than erasing it every time I turn the switch to *off*.

My hope is that these pages will demonstrate that the linguist who works with real linguistic data from real subjects, and converts those findings into numbers, must have some knowledge of statistics. Statistical tests provide us a way to determine how confident we can be about the generalizations we make. Theories abound in linguistics, but those linguists who work with data gathered in the field must be prepared to deal with what Thomas Huxley called "the great tragedy of science—the slaying of a beautiful hypothesis by an ugly fact."

I would like to thank William A. Kretzschmar, of the University of Georgia, and Michael D. Linn, of the University of Minnesota, Duluth, for their close reading of this manuscript. Bill and Mike offered much encouragement and help when I most needed them, and also made many valuable suggestions for improving the book. I also want to thank Ball State University for the assigned time I needed to complete this manuscript. Very special thanks go to Nurit, for just about everything.

Statistics in Dialectology

1. *Introduction*

Some people hate the very name of statistics, but I find them full of beauty and interest. . . . They are the only tools by which an opening can be cut through the formidable thicket of difficulties that bars the path of those who pursue the Science of Man.

Sir Francis Galton

The O.E.D. relates the term *statistics* etymologically to the Latin *status* 'a political state,' and the earliest use of the term meant the collection and description of useful data. The word still carries that meaning—we hear about "first-half statistics," the "statistics" for college enrollments, and so on. This, however, will not be the meaning of the term used here; for us, statistics will be used to describe the analysis of quantitative data—the making of inferences, based on samples, about populations from which the samples are taken. Put another way, statistical tests permit one to test limited data from a limited sample and then make inferences about the totality of all the possible observations under consideration.

Adolph Quetelet (1796-1874) is sometimes referred to as "the father of modern statistics," but one of the earliest statisticians in the modern sense was Dr. John Arbuthnot, a friend of Jonathan Swift and Alexander Pope, who, in 1710, published "An Argument for Divine Providence Taken from the Constant Regularity Observed in the Births of Both Sexes" (*Philosophical Transactions* 27:186-90). Arbuthnot's article, as its title indicates, used statistics to argue that births of nearly equal numbers of males and females could not be a function of chance alone, but rather a result of God's grand design.

1

Another early contributor to the development of statistics, in the sense that she argued strenuously for their use, was Florence Nightingale (1820-1910), who put the importance of statistical analysis in its proper perspective:

> It is by the aid of statistics that law in the social sphere can be ascertained and codified, and certain aspects of the character of God thereby revealed. The study of statistics is thus a religious service.

Francis Galton (1822-1910), quoted at the beginning of this chapter, in addition to being a cousin of Charles Darwin, can be credited with the development of correlation analysis (see Chapter 4). Karl Pearson (1857-1936) was influenced by Galton, and among his many contributions to statistical methods was his derivation, in 1910, of the chi-square distribution (See Table A-3, p. 84). The F-distribution in Table A-2 (pp. 82-83) began with the work of Sir Ronald Fisher (1890-1962). All these scholars used statistical methods, and developed new ones, in the course of their research in other fields. Fisher, for example, was a biologist by training. Karl Friedrich Gauss (1777-1855) discovered the normal distribution, sometimes called the Gaussian curve, through his research in astronomy. John Arbuthnot was a physician.

As yet, no dialectologist has made a significant, or even insignificant, contribution to statistical theory or statistical methods. In fact, these days, when statistics courses are generally required for the B.A. degree in sociology, biology, and psychology (to name only 3 fields of many), statistics is seldom a requirement for linguistics students even at the doctoral level. More than a generation has passed since Glenna Pickford 1956 criticized the *Linguistic Atlas of New England* for errors in sampling procedures, and, since then, nearly every sociolinguistic study has attempted to be more systematic in selecting subjects. Even reviews of linguistic research such as Baubkus and Viereck 1973 have tended to stress the importance of adequate and reliable sampling techniques. Regardless of the validity of Pickford's criticisms, it does seem clear that one lesson statistics has taught linguistics is that there are right and wrong ways to gather data (see Chapter 2).

What seems to be absent, however, is sufficient critical attention to the problem of analyzing the data once the sample is properly chosen. Although Levine and Crockett 1966 did use statistical testing (mainly chi-square) in their study of postvocalic /r/, the major use of statistics in dialectology began in the 1970's. Biondi 1975, Fasold 1972, Feagin 1979, and Trudgill 1974, in one way or another, all used chi-square tests to evaluate the reliability of results, and Milroy 1980 also uses a test for correlation. Ralph Fasold 1972:33, as a matter of fact, notes with some surprise that neither Labov 1966, 1969 nor Wolfram 1969 used statistical tests on their results:

> Once variability is admitted as a legitimate subject for linguistic analysis, it immediately becomes apparent that methods will be needed to distinguish truly random variability from conditioned variability. It would seem reasonable to turn to the techniques of statistical analysis, which have been designed for just such purposes. But, surprisingly, we find no examples of statistical tests having been applied to any of the data presented in Labov's work, or in the work of Wolfram (1969).

Fasold then quotes Labov's 1969 contention that, when results repeat themselves, we do not need statistical testing "to determine whether or not they might have been produced by chance." As we shall see, results are not always as clear as they at first seem to be; in fact, without statistical analysis, one is often left with mere impressions, and those impressions may or may not be valid. Moreover, we shall also find that there is always some probability that results could be a function of chance. Labov ignored the fact that statistical tests provide us with the tools to determine just how accurate our findings are; that is, they tell us at what level of probability our results, taken from a sample, allow us to make inferences about the population in question.

Crawford Feagin 1979:23 states this issue as follows:

> It is necessary to define the environments in which the variables occur, to count items, to figure percentages, to use statistics. Certain items, of course, are more amenable to counting than others, since generally the technique is to count the cases of occurrence and nonoccurrence of a certain structure. . . . It is only through such close attention to the data, rejecting impressionistic or intuitive interpretations, that it is possible to arrive at a real conception of how language works. Otherwise, we are left with hazy ideas or self-fulfilling intuitions, which distort any serious or careful (or scientific) discussion of language.

Statistical testing can aid the linguist in analyzing certain kinds of results; when the various tests are used properly, they provide an objective way to determine whether our sample results are in fact true for the population we are studying. Frank Anshen 1979:2 put the matter quite well in one short sentence: "Serious counting requires statistics." I hope that this book will demonstrate that serious dialectology requires statistics as well.

2. *Sampling*

Introductory statistics books stress the fact that only random samples are valid for making statistical inferences about the populations from which samples are taken. Since statistical analysis is based on the laws of probability, only *random samples* will do; for this reason, another term for random sample is *probability sample.*

Random samples, however, are anything but samples gathered in a haphazard manner. In fact, the classic random sample requires that everyone in the population have the same chance of being selected. If we want a sample of 50 from a population of 1,000,000, we could list all the 1,000,000 names and then choose every 20,000th name on the list. There are other techniques, involving the use of random numbers, but the basic point is that one needs a list of the members of the population to be sampled, and then must choose the sample, in some systematic fashion, from that list.

But how can we, as linguists, get such a list, even if we possessed the necessary financial resources? Not everyone pays taxes, so tax rolls are not particularly useful. Even in the United States, not everyone has a telephone, and married women are frequently listed in the telephone book under their husbands' names. Moreover, even if we surmounted all these obstacles, we might run into a problem encountered in Breathitt County, Kentucky, where a random sample originally contained a rather large number of people who were lacking full sets of front teeth, and thus were not particularly useful for phonological purposes. They were replaced, but, strictly speaking, once we add to or subtract from a random sample, it is no longer random.

Given the criteria for a random sample, we can see immediately that no major linguistic study to date has used one in the strictest sense of the word. Labov's 1966 work in New York City is frequently cited as having employed a random sample, but this is not really the case. Although he did base his sample on a sociological survey—Mobilization for Youth (MFY)—he pared that sample down from over 700 to 81 (for most of his analysis, that is). Moreover, he added 3 upper middle-class subjects who were not included in the MFY survey. Since any addition to or subtraction from a random sample automatically destroys its randomness, the statistician must conclude that there is no real justification to the claim that *The Social Stratification of English in New York City* analyzed data from a random sample. Wolfram 1969, the study of Detroit Black speech, used criteria such as clearness of the taped interview and sufficient length of the interview to select his subjects. In addition, the larger sample from which he drew his own, from the statistician's point of view, was already biased. Shuy, Wolfram, and Riley 1968 admit themselves that, since their sample in Detroit was based on elementary school children and their parents, they could not select childless couples or couples with older or younger children.

The simple fact is that any student fresh from even an introductory statistics course would find a great deal wanting in the research designs of many linguists, at least insofar as their sampling techniques are concerned. On the other hand, much the same could be said concerning other disciplines as well. Scientific research abounds with samples such as "patients treated in the month of December" or "the fifth graders at Kosciuszco School." It is hardly a secret that researchers use such samples because they are far less expensive than random ones. Satisticians unfamiliar with real-life problems, however, would sneeringly look down their noses at such samples, label them *convenience samples*, and point out that we simply cannot use any statistical tests on such samples.

What seems to be missing is a different way of understanding the notion of randomness in light of what we can learn from other scholars who are faced with problems similar to ours in the realm of subject selection. That is, unlike pure statisticians, dialectologists analyze real data from living subjects; hence one might do well to raise the question as to whether eliminating toothless people from a study of Breathitt County speech in any way biases the sample and makes it less appropriate. Put still another way, can we assume that toothless people, if they had teeth, would talk like other people of their sex and social class in Breathitt County? The answer here is affirmative, if, that is, other variables, such as social class, are not affected.

Olive Jean Dunn 1964:12 points out that

> Sometimes we have little or no choice of a sample. For example, a doctor might have given a certain type of treatment to the only twenty patients who during the last 3 years came to his office with a certain ailment. If he wishes to use these twenty patients to study the treatment he gave, he has of course been unable to choose them as a random sample from patients who might have this particular ailment. It seems reasonable, then, to consider what the population might be from which his twenty patients could be thought to be a random sample. It would perhaps be unreasonable to consider them a random sample from all patients who might have this particular ailment. If the doctor is a pediatrician whose practice is in a wealthy section of town, possibly the twenty patients might be considered as a random sample from the population of patients under 16 years of age who live in a wealthy community in this area of the country and who might have this ailment.

Theodore Colton 1977:4-7 argues that the basic question to ask is whether the *target population* (the population in the classic sense of the term) and the *sampled population* (the actual population from which the sample is drawn) can be assumed to be the same. For example, in the Detroit case cited above, the target population would be the population of Detroit, while the sampled population would be the people with children in school. If so, and this does require proof, one can make statistical inferences based on the data involved.

Seymour Sudman 1976:14 suggests the following:

> While it is useful to have census information about a defined population, this is not always possible or necessary. Studies of religious groups, criminals, and homosexuals have well-defined populations although no census material is available. . . . Most studies of criminals are done in prisons, a practice that biases the sample toward those criminals who are more likely to be arrested and convicted. Studies of homosexuals usually have been conducted in bars or with members of organized groups like the Mattachines, and are biased towards those members of the population who are most active socially. The careful studies done with these groups point out the sample deficiencies rather than attempt to revise the definition of the population.

To carry this point a bit further, we would like to be able to say that, if Kosciuszco is an upper-class girls' school in Chicago, then the speech of the children there represents a random sample of the speech of upper-class girls of comparable ages in that city. The basic point to stress here is that the burden is on us, as linguists, to demonstrate that the target population and the sample population are the same, and this burden cannot be taken lightly. Peter Trudgill's

1974 study of Norwich speech demonstrated differences between the language of working-class women who worked outside the home and that of housewives. And Michael Linn 1983:240 has also warned against choosing subjects "simply because of availability."

A further point about sampling is that one can make no statistical inferences about populations, or parts thereof, that have not been sampled. For example, Labov's 1966:4-5 claim that his sample, although taken in its entirely from Manhattan's Lower East Side, "exemplifies the complexity of New York City as a whole . . ." cannot be accepted on faith. Hans Kurath 1968:6 stated this position as follows:

> That the other parts of New York City—which includes the five boroughs of Manhattan, the Bronx, Staten Island, Brooklyn, and Queens, with a population of 8 million in an area of 320 square miles—conform to the Lower East Side of Manhattan, as Labov maintains, is more than doubtful. Can it be that Washington Heights and Harlem agree with the Lower East Side of Manhattan despite fundamental differences in social structure?

In short, we must withold judgment on the representativeness of Labov's sample until further research either supports or rejects this claim.

On the other hand, a careful reading of Labov's description of how his subjects were selected is quite convincing insofar as the question of randomness is concerned. Given his criteria for subject selection, one can argue that the New York Sample was a random sample, in the sense used here, of native speakers of English on the Lower East Side. Whether it represents the speech of New York City as a whole remains to be demonstrated.

Similarly, we can probably be confident as to the appropriateness of Roger Shuy's Detroit sample, which served as the basis for Wolfram's later study of Black speech in that city. That is, Shuy and his colleagues, as we noted earlier, sampled school children and their parents, and there seems no reason to assume that any serious bias derived from the fact that childless people and people with older children had no chance of being selected. In other words, the Detroit sample is indeed valid for statistical testing. In addition, Wolfram's requirement, among others, that there be a clear tape for analysis, hardly seems to affect the randomness of the sample. In these cases, we are on fairly solid ground if we assume that the samples are indeed random in the sense used here, and hence are valid samples for statistical testing and inference. In fact, there are significant and basic differences between research in dialectology and the kind of sampling of opinion done by Gallup, Harris, and others, and this difference was pointed out by Labov 1966:180-81:

> [L]inguistic behavior is far more general and compelling than many social attitudes or survey responses. The primary data being gathered in the New York interview are not subject to the informant's control in the way that answers on voting choices would be. . . . In studying both linguistic differentiation and linguistic evaluation, we are going beyond the self-conscious answers of the informant, to a type of behavior which he is largely unaware of.

That is, there is a fundamental difference between research in linguistics and the sampling, say, of opinions of voters. In the latter case, classic random samples are, or at least should be, the rule.

Perhaps the most frequently asked question about

samples is, "How big should one be?" Although some statistics books do provide formulas for sample size relative to population size and the levels of statistical confidence, it is rather difficult to come to a clear answer here. We do know that Gallup used somewhere between 1,500 and 2,000 for his presidential election surveys, but linguists have used far fewer. Labov used 81 for most of his analysis in New York; Wolfram used 60 in Detroit; Crawford Feagin 1979, in Anniston, Alabama, used 82; and Leslie Milroy 1980 used 46 in Belfast. More important than size, however, is how the sample is chosen. If it is chosen properly, even small samples can yield good results. The statistics used on small samples sometimes are different from those used on large ones, but in most cases they provide good bases for inferences about populations. The point is that the researcher who does not use a classic random sample must provide the reader with the sample deficiencies involved.

Ideally, one can check the validity of linguistic research that uses nonrandom samples in the classic sense by repeating the same study several times. To date, no dialectologist or sociolinguist has been sufficiently energetic to attempt this. What we are left with, then, is the fact that classic random sampling is, for all practical purposes, not really feasible for us; instead, our efforts should be spent in eliminating destructive bias, such as that involved in not sampling the speech of women who work only at home in a study of female linguistic behavior. Nondestructive bias here is defined as those factors that, to the best of our knowledge, do not influence linguistic behavior: baldness, left-handedness, a clear tape, and so on. This is hardly ideal, and probably causes some statisticians to view statistical methods in dialectology as just about as scientifically grounded as alchemy. So it goes, but then we linguists who analyze the speech of real people have known for a long time that nothing under the sun is so perfect as the world of the theoretician.

Note

1. An earlier version of this chapter was published as Davis 1986.

3. *The Frequency Distribution*

Much research in dialectology since Labov 1966 has involved the counting of the occurrences of linguistic forms. Because people tend to be inconsistent in their linguistic behavior, linguists generally find that each of their subjects pronounces a certain form a certain percentage of the time. For example, Table 3-1 shows the results of a hypothetical study of a-prefixing, where the subjects say both *I'm working* and *I'm a-working*. The percentages refer to the amount of the a-prefixed form as a fraction of the total potential places where that form could occur.

Table 3-1. % A-Prefixing in Southern Appalachia

Females % a-prefixing

Subject	Age	%
1	34	47
2	31	32
3	42	16
4	30	25
6	31	68
7	40	14
8	38	56
9	29	25
10	27	70

$n_1 = 10$ Total % = 400

Males % a-prefixing

Subject	Age	%
11	42	49
12	28	73
13	43	29

14	32	57
15	31	67
16	27	93
17	36	18
18	40	25
19	33	76
20	29	83

$n_2 = 10$ Total % = 570

The mean, or arithmetic average, of the data in Table 3-1 is calculated by adding all the percentages for the men and the women (400 [women] + 570 [men]), and then dividing that sum (970) by the total number of subjects ($n_1 + n_2 = 20$). In this case $970/20 = 48.5$. In most cases, however, linguists want to make comparisons, so we can also calculate the means for the women and men separately. In this case, we divide the total percentages for the groups by the number of subjects in each. Since we have 10 in each group, the mean for the women is 40 and that for the men is 57.

Means, of and by themselves, however, are hardly sufficient evidence for the conclusion that, in the population under consideration, men exhibit more a-prefixing than women. Perhaps the results in Table 3-1 are true only for our sample. We also need to know how homogeneous the data are, and, to find this out, we calculate the standard deviations of these two means. The standard deviation (s) is extremely useful, since, given the laws of probability, we can predict the number of observations that should fall within various numbers of standard deviations from the mean.

For example, if we have a sample with a mean of 125 and a standard deviation of 12, then, given the laws of probability, 68% of all the cases in our frequency distribution should fall somewhere between 113 (125 − 12) and 137 (125 + 12). Similarly, approximately two standard deviations (actually 1.96) left and right of the mean cover 95% of the scores or, in this case, from 101 (125 − 24) to 149 (125 + 24). This property of s, as we shall see, is quite useful; it means that if we obtain results that are more than 1.96 standard deviations from the mean, we can be 95% certain that these results are valid for the population that we are studying. We will return to the concept of this decision rule in Chapter 4.

The standard deviation (s) is calculated using the following formula:

$$\sqrt{\frac{\Sigma (O - m)^2}{n - 1}}$$

The *sigma* (Σ) always means "add up whatever follows." In this case, we must subtract the mean (m) from each observation (O) in the frequent distribution in Table 3-1, square the result, add up all the squares, and divide by one less than the number of people in each sample. Then we calculate the square root of that result. Table 3-2 shows the calculation of the standard deviation for the women in Table 3–1, where the mean percent of a-prefixing was 40.

Table 3-2. Standard Deviation for Women

Females	% a-prefixing	O - m	$(O - m)^2$
1	47	7	49
2	32	-8	64
3	16	−24	576
4	25	−15	225
5	47	7	49
6	68	28	784
7	14	−26	676
8	56	16	256
9	25	−15	225
10	70	30	900

$$\Sigma (O - m)^2 = 3,804$$

$$s = \sqrt{\frac{\Sigma (O - m)^2}{n - 1}} = \sqrt{\frac{3,804}{9}} = 20.559$$

The calculation of s for the men is shown in Table 3-3.

Table 3-3. Standard Deviation for Men

Males	% a-prefixing	O - m	$(O - m)^2$
11	49	–8	64
12	73	16	256
13	29	–28	784
14	57	0	0
15	67	10	100
16	93	36	1,296
17	18	–39	1,521
18	25	–32	1,024
19	76	19	361
20	83	26	676

$$\Sigma(O - m)^2 = 6,082$$

$$s = \sqrt{\frac{\Sigma (O - m)^2}{n - 1}} = \sqrt{\frac{6,082}{9}} = 25.996$$

As we shall see later, we can use these means and standard deviations to test whether the difference of 17 percentage points between the means of the women and the men is significant or is, instead, merely a function of the two samples involved and not valid for the population as a whole. The square of s (s^2) is called the *variance*. It will be discussed in Chapter 4.2.

The setting up of a frequency distribution such as that in

Table 3-1 should always be the first step in the analysis of quantitative linguistic data. Once all the data are collected, comparisons can be made between males and females, age groups, socioeconomic classes, and so on. In some cases, such as comparing the scores of the sexes, the grouping is natural: males and females. In the case of the social class, however, such is seldom the case. Since many linguists now use a numerical scale to rank their subjects, they have to decide on the number of classes appropriate for their samples. To illustrate this, we can examine the techniques used by Wolfram 1969, who used 3 criteria to determine the social class of his subjects: education, occupation, and residence.

For example, a teacher with a college degree who lived in a 5-room flat would be ranked as follows:

	Rating	Multiplication Factor	Weighted Score
Education	2	5	10
Occupation	2	9	18
Residence	3	6	18

Total Social Status Score = 46

One of Wolfram's scales—education—is listed below:

Rating	Level of Education
1	any graduate degree
2	college education
3	one year or more of college
4	high school education
5	some high school (tenth grade)
6	junior high school
7	less than seven years (p. 33)

Wolfram had similar scales for occupation and residence. He gave each subject a social class score, and those scores

17

ranged from 20 (the highest social class score) to 134 (the lowest).

Table 3-4 presents the results (for illustrative purposes only) of a sociolinguistic study of a glottal stop realization of /t/ in words such as *water* and *bottle*. This study used similar social scales to Wolfram's, so the subjects' socioeconomic ranks (SEC Rank) and their actual scores for glottal stop realization of /t/ (% [ʔ]) are both listed:

Table 3-4. Class Rank and /t/ Realization

Subject	SEC Rank	% [ʔ]
1	30	15
2	37	25
3	57	20
4	61	10
5	69	70
6	72	35
7	91	20
8	103	40
9	123	100
10	125	80
11	127	20
12	130	10
13	131	15
14	132	60
15	156	80
16	156	65
17	167	65
18	168	60
19	185	10
20	205	85

Assuming that we have already decided on 4 classes, we could quite reasonably divide the subjects into the following more or less "natural" groups, from the highest social class to the lowest. Class widths (the size of each class) are also listed:

Class	Ranks(class width)	No. of Subjects
1	30-61	4
2	69-103	4
3	123-132	6
4	156-205	6

We would then get the following means for [?]:

Class	Mean % [?]
1	17.50
2	41.25
3	47.50
4	60.83

These results are neat indeed. We can show the occurrence of increasingly more nonstandard forms as socioeconomic class becomes lower. We have here a classic case of what Labov 1966 termed "fine stratification" of the variable.

Suppose, on the other hand, that we decide to divide the subjects in Table 3-4 into 4 equal groups of 5 each: 1-5, 6-10, 11-15, and 16-20. Now the means for the 4 classes are as follows:

Class	Class Width	Mean % [?]
1	30-69	31
2	72-125	55
3	127-132	37
4	156-205	57

Unlike the former case, we can now use these data to show a kind of roller-coaster effect, with similarities between classes 1 and 3 on one hand and 2 and 4 on the other. However, the differences in the class widths hardly justify such a procedure, because the socioeconomic class scores are very unevenly distributed. Class 3, in fact, has a class width of only 6, whereas class 2 has a class width of 54.

To solve the problem of unequal class widths, we could take the total range of socioeconomic rank scores (30 to 205) and divide that range (175) by the number of classes (4). The result is 43.75, and, if we use 43 as our class width, we get the following 4 social classes:

Class	Class Width	No. of Subjects
1	33-73	6
2	74-117	2
3	118-161	8
4	162-205	4

Of course, our subjects now are quite unevenly distributed, but if we do calculate the means for the 4 social classes we get the following:

Class	Mean % [?]
1	29.17
2	30.00
3	53.75
4	55.00

Now we can show, again in Labov's 1966 terms, "sharp stratification" between the upper 2 groups and the lower 2. In other words, depending on one's decision about dividing subjects into social classes, it appears that it is easy enough to support a rather wide variety of hypotheses about the linguistic data gathered.

In some cases, as noted earlier, no problems or pitfalls exist. For example, if one compares females and males, subjects from New York and London, Roman Catholics and Jews, or blacks and whites, the question of grouping does not arise. It arises only when the classes are determined along a continuous scale. At this point, it is essential to find an objective criterion for establishing social class distinctions, and the linguist may feel that there is no choice but to turn to nonlinguistic data, usually in the form of sociological surveys.

To make this point clearer, one can examine some of Labov's 1966 methods of analysis. Using quantitative methods, Labov arrived at 10 groups of subjects, listed here from the lowest (0) to the highest (9):

Group	No. of Subjects
0	7
1	7
2	9
3	13
4	10
5	5
6	8
7	9
8	2
9	11

Labov divided these groups into 3 classes. The following list shows the relative percentages of Labov's classes, compared with the Mobilization for Youth (MFY) classes, the random sample from which Labov chose the major part of his sample (he did add 3 subjects not on the MFY list in order to bring his highest class—9—up from 8 subjects to 11). Labov's decision to divide his subjects into 3 social classes seems to have been motivated by previous sociological research. As we can see, Labov's classes match very well with the larger sample from which his own was taken:

Subjects	% Labov's Subjects	% MFY
Lower (0-2)	28	30
Working (3-5)	35	33

In his analysis of postvocalic /r/ constriction, Labov obtained the following percents for the 3 classes:

	n	Casual (A)	Careful (B)	Reading (C)
(0-2)	23	2.5	10.5	14.5
(3-5)	28	4.0	12.5	29.0
(6-9)	30	12.0	25.0	29.0

	Word Lists (D)	Minimal Pairs (D')
(0-2)	23.5	49.5
(3-5)	35.0	55.0
(6-9)	55.0	70.0

These results are graphed in Figure 3-1, showing, in Labov's terms, fine stratification of the variable.

Figure 3-1. Postvocalic /r/ Distribution

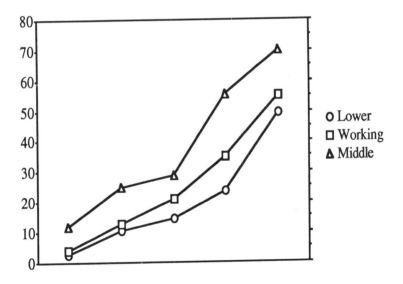

Later in the analysis, however, Labov argues that a graph similar to that presented here as Figure 3-1 suggests the "half-truth that (r) stratifies the population into three distinct class groups" (Labov 1966:237). In order to present a supposedly clearer picture, Labov changes his 3 classes into 6: 0, 1, 2–3, 4–5, 6–8, and 9.

Class 6-8, Labov's lower middle class, exhibits what he calls a "crossover pattern," exhibiting 20% more /r/ constriction for minimal pairs than class 9, the highest. He then argues that this demonstrates the lower middle class's linguistic insecurity at the more formal style levels. Since he believes that "the middle class group 6-9 is not a coherent unit with respect to (r)," he divides that group into 6-8 on the one hand and 9 on the other.

One perfectly legitimate question to raise about Labov's method here is what motivated his decision to change his class groupings? That is, what justification did Labov have for suggesting that the results in Figure 3-1 suggest half truths, when those results are based on social class distinctions arrived at by a sociological survey?

The fact is that Labov's decision to change his classes, here and in other parts of his classic study of New York City speech, suggests a certain circularity of reasoning. He used linguistic criteria for deciding that "the middle class group 6-9 is not a coherent unit with respect to (r)," yet one of the goals of the study was to shed light on the relationship between linguistic variety and social class.

Put another way, Labov's hypothesis about hypercorrection and the crossover pattern is supported by the manipulation of his social class categories. Given the absence of any sociological basis for changing the groups, however, the only conclusion possible is that these results may not be valid for the social classes of New York City, or, more precisely, of the Lower East Side, from which the sample was drawn.

23

Moreover, Labov's redefined classes are unevenly distributed insofar as the number of subjects in each class. Classes 0 and 1 contain 7 subjects each; class 2-3 contains 16; class 4-5 contains 14; class 6-8 contains 19, and class 9 contains 11. The results are neat and support Labov's hypotheses, but neat is all they are. Other groupings would have given other results, and certainly the burden is on the linguist to justify the methods (s)he uses.

We have seen that there can be several perfectly logical and defensible ways to divide subjects into groups, and the decision on the groupings themselves may sometimes determine the results. Moreover, we cannot rely totally on sociological studies because (1) sometimes they do not exist for a particular problem, (2) sometimes they may be outdated, and (3) sometimes their reliability is questionable.

For these reasons, we would be wise to avoid grouping subjects into classes based on quantitative scales. Instead, when subjects, as in Table 3-4, receive a particular score as part of a socioeconomic class index, we should calculate the *coefficient of correlation* to determine if there indeed is a relationship between socioeconomic class score and the linguistic variable in question.

The coefficient of correlation is relatively easy to calculate and will be discussed in Chapter 4.5. When used, it tells us whether there is a relationship between two sets of data, such as those in Table 3-4 above, and at what level of statistical significance (see below) the relationship exists. We can do this without dividing the subjects into groups and thus can eliminate the risks outlined above.[2]

As it turns out, the coefficient of correlation for the data in Table 3-1, does permit us to say that a relationship exists between [?] use and social class rank. The important point here is that linguists must strive for objectivity; although our graphs and tables (and our conclusions as well) may turn out to be a bit less neat sometimes, our research just might bear better the test of scientific scrutiny.

Notes

1. Earlier versions of sections of this chapter were published in Davis 1982, 1985, and 1986.
2. Because it reveals only linear relationships, the coefficient of correlation will not reveal the kind of bimodal distribution found by Levine and Crockett 1966, or, for that matter, a relationship that holds for only part of a speech community. Such situations, one hopes, would be revealed by other testing.

4. *Testing Linguistic Data*

4.1 Comparison of Means: Large Samples

If we set up a frequency distribution and calculate the means of two samples, how can we be certain that our results are valid for the population under study? In other words, even if we were to sample as many as 5,000 people from the population of London, the sample would be quite a small percentage of the total population. We must be able to show that our results are valid for our population and not only for the sample itself. Certainly a term such as *valid* is relative, so a better way to phrase this question is, "How valid, or how significant, are the results?" Statistics provide a fairly exact answer to this question and phrase it in the following way: "What is the probability that the results are a function of sample behavior alone, and not of population behavior?" Statisticians refer to this formulation as the *null hypothesis*. The question that we ask, then, is whether we can reject the null hypothesis and at what level of probability.

Suppose, for example, we desire to compare men's and women's pronunciations of postvocalic /r/ constriction in a reading passage, and we obtained the following results:

$$\text{men } (n_1 = 100) \qquad m_1 = 24 \qquad s_1 = 4$$
$$\text{women } (n_2 = 50) \qquad m_2 = 22 \qquad s_2 = 5$$

That is, the mean for the 100 men is 24%, with a standard deviation (*s*) of 4, while the mean for the 50 women is 22%, with an *s* of 5. The null hypotheses is that there is no significant difference between the women and the men insofar as their use of postvocalic /r/ constriction. Statistics provide the tools that permit us to determine the statistical significance, as defined above, of the 2 percentage points difference between the means, rather than our relying on intuitions alone.[1] First, we calculate s_D, the standard error of difference between the two means:

$$s_D = \sqrt{\frac{s_1^2}{n_1} + \frac{s_1^2}{n_2}}$$

That is, we square the two standard deviations, divide each by the number in their respective samples, add those results, then take the square root of the sum. In the above case of postvocalic /r/, we get the following results:

$$s_D = \sqrt{\frac{4^2}{100} + \frac{5^2}{50}} = \sqrt{\frac{16}{100} + \frac{25}{50}} = .812$$

Now, we divide the difference between the means of the men and the women $(24 - 22 = 2)$ by s_D:

$$z = \frac{24 - 22}{.812} = 2.463$$

This z is the number of standard deviations on either side of the mean in which our results are included. Given modern statistical tables, we have little problem in interpreting results in standard deviations. Suppose, for example, our results were 1.960 standard deviations. If you look at Table A-1 (p. 81), you note that the left-hand column lists "degrees of freedom." This term will be explained later, but, for now, look at the last degree of freedom, which has the infinity symbol (∞). Now find 1.960 in the row next to the ∞ and run your finger to the top of that column, where you will see .05, meaning that there is a 5% probability that our results are *not* significant for the population we are studying. If we had obtained a result of 2.576, the table tells us that there would be only a 1% probability that our results were a function only of sample behavior and not population behavior. 3.291 would have been still better, since there would have been only one-tenth of a percent (.001) probability that our results could have happened by chance.

Since our calculated z (2.463) is more than 1.960 but less than 2.576, we say that our results are valid at $p < .05$. (Here, and in every case, we always choose the lower probability.) This means that there is less than a 5% probability that the difference between the means of the men and the women for postvocalic /r/ constriction is a function of chance—of the people sampled for the study, and not of the population of men and women under consideration.

We have already noted that statisticians generally state problems in terms of the *null hypothesis*. That is, they ask, "What is the probability that the results obtained are a function of chance, of sample behavior, rather than of population behavior?" In the above case, the null hypothesis would be that there is no difference between the males and the females in the population in question regarding the way they pronuonce postvocalic /r/. Our results, then, allow us to reject the null hypothesis (abbreviated H_O), that the means of the men and women are equal, at a level of significance of $p < .05$. In other words, there is still a 5% probability that our results are not significant for the population that we are studying.

This 5% probability associated with a z of 1.96 is usually the minimum required for research in the social sciences. Had our z been equal to or higher than 2.576, we could have rejected H_O at $p < .01$, with only a 1% probability that our inference is invalid about the population from which the samples were drawn. At $p < .001$, where z is greater than or equal to 3.291, there is a probability of 1 in 1,000 that an inference is not valid. Since tradition in the social sciences has generally settled on $p < .05$, a linguist probably should consult a good applied statistician before accepting significance levels above $p < .05$ (such as $p < .10$ or $p < .15$) as evidence for rejecting H_O.

The above test for the difference between 2 means can be

28

used only when samples are large. "Large" here usually can be interpreted as more than 30 (n > 30), for reasons which are outside the scope of this book. It is instructive, however, to see what happens when the samples, though still large, become considerably smaller. We can use the means of the women and men for postvocalic /r/ constriction on page 26, but this time change the sample sizes. All else remains the same:

$$\text{men } (n_1 = 32) \qquad m_1 = 24 \qquad s_1 = 4$$
$$\text{women } (n_2 = 33) \qquad m_2 = 22 \qquad s_2 = 5$$

$$s_D = \sqrt{\frac{16^2}{32} + \frac{25^2}{33}} = 1.121$$

$$z = \frac{24 - 22}{1.121} = 1.784$$

Now, p > .05 (is greater than .05), and we cannot reject the null hypothesis this time; the sample sizes make the difference. Levels of significance are a function of several factors: the actual difference between the means, the standard deviations, and sample size. For example, large standard deviations result in a larger s_D and cause the resulting z to be smaller. Unless one has a wealth of experience in statistical analysis, one generally cannot arrive intuitively at the level of significance at which results are significant. Findings almost never speak for themselves; they require a statistical interpretation before inferences from samples can be made about the populations from which the samples are drawn.

To take another example, Wald and Shopen 1981:237 studied, among other things, the difference between the linguistic behavior of males and females regarding the pronunciation of (ING) ([faitin], as opposed to [faitiŋ]):

$$\text{men } (n_1 = 47) \qquad m_1 = 24.4 \qquad s_1 = 20.4$$
$$\text{women } (n_2 = 33) \qquad m_2 = 15.6 \qquad s_2 = 16.4$$

$$s_D = \sqrt{\frac{20.4^2}{47} + \frac{16.4^2}{33}} = 4.124$$

$$z = \frac{24.4 - 15.6}{4.124} = 2.134$$

We now know that the difference between the means of the females and the males is valid at a level of significance of $p < .05$, because z is greater than 1.96 but less than 2.575 $(2.575 > z > 1.96)$.

This test is valid only when the data are continuous. *Continuous data* are those which can be cut down into smaller and smaller units, such as, for example, the age of a person. (S)he can be 25 years old, or 25 years and 8 months, or 25 years, 8 months, 3 weeks, 4 days, 6 hours, 12 minutes, 52.78943 seconds and so on. Noncontinuous data can be exemplified by the number of universities in England, the number of people in a room, and so on. When the data are noncontinuous, one can use the Mann-Whitney test, which will be explained in the next section.

4.2 Comparison of Means: Small Samples

We noted above that, for our purposes, we can use the number 30 as the dividing point between large samples and small ones. The test for the difference between means outlined above is appropriate for large samples only, so we need another procedure for small samples, such as those in Table 3-1. We noted there that m_2 (women) = 40 and that m_1 (men) = 57. The standard deviations are $s_2 = 20.559$ and $s_1 = 25.996$. In principle, the test for the difference between the means of 2 small samples is the same as that for large samples. The difference is that we calculate s_D

30

differently:

$$s_D = \sqrt{\frac{(n_1 - 1) s_1^2 + (n_1 - 1) s_2^2}{n_1 + n_2 - 2}} \sqrt{\frac{1}{n_1} + \frac{1}{n_2}}$$

The calculations for the data in Table 3-1 are as follows:

$$s_D = \sqrt{\frac{(10 - 1) \, 20.559^2 + (10 - 1) \, 25.996^2}{10 + 10 - 2}} \sqrt{\frac{1}{10} + \frac{1}{10}}$$
$$= 23.436 \text{ x } .447 = 10.476$$

Now, we proceed as with large samples, and divide the difference between the means by s_D :

$$t = \frac{40 - 57}{10.476} = -1.623$$

Here, as with z, the minus sign is not relevant for us. The statistic t is different from z, in that the former is used for small samples. To evaluate the calculated t, we must use the "t-Distribution Table," produced here as Table A-1 on page 81. Along the left margin of the table, we find *degrees of freedom* (df). We calculate the degrees of freedom for small samples as follows:

$$df = (n_1 - 1) + (n_2 - 1)$$

So df for the above problem is $(10 - 1) + (10 - 1) = 18$. If we check the row next to 18 degrees of freedom, and match it with the column under .05, we see that, at df $= 18$, t must equal at least 2.101 for us to reject the null hypothesis at p < .05. Since our calculated t is only 1.623, we cannot say that there is a significant difference between males and females insofar as a-prefixing is concerned. Indeed, another look at Table A-1 reveals that H_0 can be rejected only at p <

31

.25 (1.623 is larger than the 1.330 of p < .25 but smaller than the 1.734 of p < .10), so we are well above the minimum confidence level of p < .05 generally used in the social sciences. This test for differences between means of small samples is usually called the "t-test," and it can also be used on the following data:

Mean Final Consonant Cluster Deletion:
Lower Middle Class

$$\text{children } (n_1 = 12) \quad m_1 = 73 \quad s_1 = 10$$
$$\text{adults } (n_2 = 12) \quad m_2 = 63 \quad s_2 = 8$$

$$s_D = \sqrt{\frac{(12-1)\,10^2 + (12-1)\,8^2}{12 + 12 - 2}} \sqrt{\frac{1}{12} + \frac{1}{12}}$$

$$= 3.697$$

$$t = \frac{73 - 63}{3.697} = 2.705$$

Here df = 22, since $(12 - 1) + (12 - 1) = 22$, and Table A-1 indicates that we can reject H_o at p < .05. The calculated t value is greater than 2.508, but it is less than 2.819 (p < .01). Now we can say that the difference between mean final consonant cluster deletion of children and adults of the population in question is significant at p < .05. Muller 1968:229 cites the following data—the number of milliseconds it took for Frenchmen and French Canadians to pronounce a certain word:

French (n = 7)

1 134
2 161
3 170

```
          4  162
          5  179
          6  164
          7  142
```

French Canadians (n = 7)

```
          8  125
          9  127
         10  121
         11  124
         12  156
         13  139
         14  146
```

French	Canadians
$m_1 = 158.86$	$m_2 = 134.00$
$s_1 = 15.67$	$s_2 = 13.24$
$s_1^2 = 245.55$	$s_2^2 = 175.30$

$$s_D = \sqrt{\frac{(6 \times 245.55) + (6 \times 175.30)}{12}} \; \sqrt{\frac{1}{7} + \frac{1}{7}}$$

$$= 7.743$$

$$t = \frac{158.86 - 134.00}{7.743} = 3.211$$

According to Table A-1, our calculated t, at df = 12, indicates a level of significance of $p < .01$, so we can reject the null hypothesis and say that Frenchmen did indeed pronounce the word slower than French Canadians did. In fact, there is only 1 chance in 100 that we are wrong. The question of the scientific significance of .002486 seconds is strictly a linguistic matter, not a statistical one.

Many statisticians, however, have argued that the t-test is based on certain assumptions about the nature of the data being analyzed. One is that the data be continuous (see p. 30). Another such assumption is that both of the samples used for comparison must come from normally distributed populations with equal *variances*, the squares of the standard deviations of the two samples. One must demonstrate this before applying the t-test. To illustrate this procedure, let us assume that we obtained the following results for the number of mistakes in a 300-word English composition, written by native speakers of French and German:

$$\text{French } (n_1 = 13) \qquad m_1 = 46 \qquad s_1 = 23$$
$$\text{German } (n_2 = 11) \qquad m_2 = 35 \qquad s_2 = 20$$

$$s_1^2 = 529$$

$$s_2^2 = 400$$

First, we take the 2 variances, and divide the smaller into the larger:

$$F = \frac{529}{400} = 1.322$$

Table A-2, on pages 82-83, is called the *F-Distribution*. It contains values for both the numerator and denominator, which are simply the number of subjects in each sample, minus 1. For the above problem, the numerator is $13 - 1 = 12$ (French) and the denominator is $11 - 1 = 10$ (German). (We could just have easily reversed these; it makes no difference.) When we test variances, we generally write $F_{A/B}$, meaning the F-score of the numerator (A) over the denominator (B). Table A-2 shows that $F_{12/10} = 2.91$ at p $< .05$ (the light-colored type). We also have to reverse the process and calculate $F_{B/A}$. Table A-2 indicates that, with a (now) numerator of 10 and a denominator of 12, F = 2.76. Then we take the reciprocal of that: 1/2.76 = 0.362. Our total F values are as follows:

$$F_{\underline{A}} = 2.91 \text{ (from Table A-2)}$$
$$_{B}$$

$$\frac{1}{F_{\underline{B}}} = \frac{1}{2.76} = 0.362$$
$$\phantom{\frac{1}{F}}_{A}$$

Since, when we divided the smaller variance into the larger, our result was 1.322, and since that falls between 2.91 and 0.362, we can say that the variances of the two samples are "equal," and that the *t*-test may be performed on the data. When we do so, incidentally, $t = 1.184$, so $p < .50$, which is far from allowing us to reject the null hypothesis.

Now consider the following frequency distribution:

Table 4-1. % Postvocalic /r/ in Free Conversation

Boys	Girls
12	12
0	17
65	18
87	20
60	57
81	22
30	17
84	42
0	19
72	18
0	12
10	20

If we perform a *t*-test on these data, we get the following results:

$$s_D = \sqrt{\frac{(11 \times 36.21^2) + (11 \times 13.20^2)}{12 \times 12 \times 12}} \quad \sqrt{\frac{1}{12} + \frac{1}{12}}$$

$$= 11.126$$

$$t = \frac{41.75 - 22.83}{11.126} = 1.701$$

This means that we cannot reject H_0 at $p < .05$, since, at df $= 22$, Table A-1 indicates that our t value is significant only at $p < .25$. However, a difficulty arises because of the great difference between the standard deviations of the two samples (36.21 for the boys, as opposed to 13.20 for the girls). The test for variances reveals the following:

$$F = \frac{36.21^2}{13.20^2} = 7.525$$

Table A-2 shows that, at $p < .05$, $F_{A/B} = 2.82$. The numerator and the denominator are the same here (11), because the samples are of equal size (12), so

$$\frac{1}{F_{\frac{B}{A}}} = \frac{1}{2.82} = 0.355$$

Now we see that our calculated F value of 7.525 falls outside the range of 2.82 to 0.355, so the data from the two samples are not comparable and we cannot use the t-test.

On the other hand, several modern statisticians have argued that, if the two samples are of equal or nearly equal size, the t-test can be used without testing variances. In fact, Box 1953 suggests that the t-test is so powerful (robust is the term used in statistics) that to "make the preliminary test on variances is rather like putting out to sea in a rowing boat to find out whether conditions are sufficiently calm for an ocean liner to leave port" (quoted in Zar 1974:107).

Other statisticians, however, still argue for the F-test. Fortunately, there are other tests we can apply, rather than simply relying on the opinion of this statistician or that. These other tests for the differences between means do not require identical variances and can be used on noncontinuous data. They are called *nonparametric tests*. One of the best-known of these is the Mann-Whitney test, which involves ranking the scores of the subjects. To see how it works, we can use the data in Table 4-1.

First, we rank the scores for the 24 subjects from the lowest to the highest. Here, n_1 = boys and n_2 = girls, but it makes no difference as to which is which. In the case of ties (3 children have 0%, 3 have 12%, etc.), we take the average of those ranks. For example, since 3 subjects scored 0%, we take the first 3 ranks (1, 2, and 3), add them (= 6), and divide by the number of ranks (3). All 3 subjects, then, get the rank of 2. The 10% score is the next highest, so that subject, a boy, is ranked number 4. There are 3 scores of 12%, so we add the ranks 5, 6, and 7 (= 18), and divide by 3 (= 6). The 3 children who scored 12% all get the rank of 6. This ranking procedure continues until each score receives a rank:

Boys	Girls	Rank of Boys	Rank of Girls
12	12	6	6
0	17	2	8.5
65	18	20	10.5
87	20	24	13.5
60	57	19	18
81	22	22	15
30	17	16	8.5
84	42	23	17
0	19	2	12
72	18	21	10.5

0	12	2	6
20	10	4	13.5

$$n_1 = 12 \quad n_2 = 12 \quad R_1 = 161 \quad R_2 = 139$$

Now we calculate the statistic U, for the Mann-Whitney test:

$$U = n_1 \, n_2 + \frac{n_1 \, (n_1 + 1)}{2} - R_1$$

In the case of the above problem, the calculation is as follows:

$$U = (12 \times 12) + \frac{12 \, (12 + 1)}{2} - 161 = 61$$

The z value can then be determined by the following formula:[2]

$$z = \frac{U - \dfrac{n_1 \, n_2}{2}}{\sqrt{\dfrac{n_1 \, n_2 \, (n_1 + n_2 + 1)}{12}}} = \frac{61 - \dfrac{144}{2}}{\sqrt{\dfrac{(12 \times 12) \, (12 \times 12 + 1)}{12}}}$$

$$= \frac{-11}{17.32} = -.6351$$

Since z is far below 1.96, we cannot reject H_O at $p < .05$, and the Mann-Whitney test supports the findings of the t-test. We now see that the t-test worked, in spite of the large difference between the variances of the two samples. We should also note that, in spite of the fact that the mean for the boys is nearly twice that of the girls, we cannot regard that difference as significant—another demonstration of the fact that linguistic data cannot speak for themselves. They require statistical interpretation.

4.3 Comparison of 2 Percentages: The Proportion Test

We can state categorically that, whenever possible, linguistic data should be analyzed according to the procedures outlined above. That is, one should always set up frequency distributions and calculate the means and standard deviations of the samples involved. If the variances are widely disparate, one can use nonparametric tests, but these too are based on frequency distributions.

Not always, however, can we set up frequency distributions. Consider the following data:

% Subjects Using Multiple Negation
men ($n_1 = 50$) 60% (p_1)
women ($n_2 = 56$) 50% (p_2)

Here, no frequency distribution is possible. Each subject either used multiple negation or did not do so, and the statistical test on these data is different. First we calculate *pi* (π):

$$\pi = \frac{n_1\,p_1 + n_2\,p_2}{n_1 + n_2}$$

$$= \frac{(50 \times .60) + (56 \times .50)}{50 + 56} = .547$$

The next step is the calculation of z:

$$z = \frac{p_1 - p_2}{\sqrt{\pi\,(1 - \pi)\left(\dfrac{1}{n_1} + \dfrac{1}{n_2}\right)}}$$

$$= \frac{.60 - .50}{\sqrt{(.547)(.543)\left(\frac{1}{60} + \frac{1}{50}\right)}}$$

$$= \frac{.10}{\sqrt{.009}} = \frac{.10}{.095} = 1.053$$

Since our z is less than 1.96, we cannot reject H_o, and must conclude that, given our decision to use the $p < .05$ level of probability, the difference in the use of multiple negation by the men and women cannot be regarded as population behavior; rather, we must regard it as likely to be sample behavior only.

This proportion test can be used only when samples are large ($n > 30$). It is worth noting what would happen if the same results were obtained from much larger samples. In the example below, the percentages stay the same ($p_1 = .60$, $p_2 = .50$), but sample sizes are different—much larger:

% Subjects Using Multiple Negation
men ($n_1 = 200$) 60% (p_1)
women ($n_2 = 300$) 50% (p_2)

$$\pi = \frac{n_1 p_1 + n_2 p_2}{n_1 + n_2} = \frac{(200 \times .60) + (300 \times .50)}{200 + 300} = .540$$

$$z = \frac{p_1 - p_2}{\sqrt{\pi (1 - \pi)\left(\frac{1}{n_1} + \frac{1}{n_2}\right)}}$$

$$= \frac{.60 - .50}{\sqrt{(.540)(.460)\left(\frac{1}{200} + \frac{1}{300}\right)}}$$

$$= \frac{.10}{.045} = 2.222$$

Now our z is larger than 1.96. With larger samples, then, $p < .05$. As we have seen previously, the numbers just do not speak for themselves. We need statistical testing to interpret them.

In Chapter 1, we observed that Labov's 1966 work on New York City speech did not employ statistical testing. In his well-known department store survey, Labov noted that, at Saks Fifth Avenue, the most prestigious of the 3 stores, the employees' pronunciation of *fourth* ran from 30% postvocalic /r/ constriction in the casual style to 40% in the emphatic style. Had he tested these results, he would have found the following:

$$\pi = \frac{n_1\,p_1 + n_2\,p_2}{n_1 + n_2} = \frac{(200 \times .60) + (300 \times .50)}{200 + 300} = .540$$

$$z = \frac{p_1 - p_2}{\sqrt{\pi\,(1 - \pi)\left(\frac{1}{n_1} + \frac{1}{n_2}\right)}}$$

$$= \frac{.30 - .40}{\sqrt{(.3113)\,(.6887)\left(\frac{1}{56} + \frac{1}{40}\right)}} = 1.0438$$

In other words, one cannot reject the null hypothesis at $p < .05$, yet this 10% difference between style levels is the largest one in the department store survey. Based on these results then, we can state that Labov did not demonstrate at $p < .05$ that "casual" and "emphatic" represent two different style levels in the stores studied.

On the other hand, the proportion test on the data from Saks Fifth Avenue and Macy's does reveal a social class difference for *floor* at the so-called casual style:

Saks ($n_1 = 49$) $p_1 = .63$
Macy's ($n_2 = 110$) $p_2 = .40$

$$\pi = \frac{(49 \times .63) + (110 \times .40)}{49 + 110} = .680$$

$$z = \frac{.63 - .40}{\sqrt{(.680)(.320)\left(\frac{1}{49} + \frac{1}{110}\right)}} = \frac{.19}{.080} = 2.375$$

Therefore: $p < .025$

4.4 Analysis of More than 2 Percentages: Chi-Square

Perhaps the best known of all statistical tests is the nonparametric test, chi-square (X^2). Generally speaking, it can be used to test the relationship of several percentages; that is, we can test the null hypothesis that there is no relationship in the following table between educational level and the responses to Received Pronunciation (RP):

EDUCATIONAL LEVEL

Response	Primary	Secondary	College	Total
Positive	72	400	201	673
Neutral	20	123	56	209
Negative	8	77	43	128
Total	100	600	300	1,000

Of the total 1,000 subjects, 673 (67.3%) responded positively to RP, 128 (12.8%) responded negatively and 209 (20.9%) were neutral. If these scores were not a function of education, we would expect that, for example, 67.3% of the 100 subjects with a primary school education would respond positively, 67.3% of those with a secondary school education would respond positively and so on. The following table presents the calculations for these "expected" scores:

42

	Primary	Secondary	College
Pos.	100 x.673=67.3	600 x.673=403.8	300 x.673=201.9
Neut.	100 x.209=20.9	600 x.209=125.4	300 x .209=62.7
Neg.	100 x.128=12.8	600 x .128 = 76.8	300 x .128=38.4

We can list the actual scores and the expected scores. The latter are in parentheses:

	Primary	Secondary	College
Positive	72 (67.3)	400 (403.8)	201 (201.9)
Neutral	20 (20.9)	123 (125.4)	56 (62.7)
Negative	8 (12.8)	77 (76.8)	43 (38.4)

Now we calculate X^2, which involves subtracting the expected score from the actual score, squaring that difference, dividing by the expected score, and adding all those results. The formula is as follows:

$$X^2 = \sum \frac{(\text{actual - expected})^2}{\text{expected}}$$

For the response to RP, then, the calculation is as follows:

$$X^2 = \frac{(72 - 67.3)^2}{67.3} + \frac{(400 - 403.8)^2}{403.83} + \frac{(201 - 201.9)^2}{201.9}$$

$$+ \frac{(20 - 20.9)^2}{20.9} + \frac{(123 - 125.4)^2}{125.4} + \frac{(56 - 62.7)^2}{62.7}$$

$$+ \frac{(8 - 12.8)^2}{12.8} + \frac{(77 - 76.8)^2}{76.8} + \frac{(43 - 38.4)^2}{38.4}$$

$$= .328 + .036 + .044$$

$$+ .039 + .046 + .716$$

43

$$+ 1.80 + .042 + .551$$

$$= 3.562$$

Our calculated $X^2 = 3.562$. To find the level of significance, we turn to the X^2 *Distribution Table*, presented here as Table A-3 on page 84. Along the left margin of the table, we find degrees of freedom (as was the case with the *t*-test). For X^2, degrees of freedom are calculated as follows:

$$df = (r - 1) (c - 1)$$

where "r" stands for horizontal rows and "c" stands for vertical columns. Since we have 3 rows and 3 columns in our problem, df = (3 - 1) (3 - 1) = 4. Table A-3 tells us that, at df = 4, X^2 must equal at least 9.488 for the results to be significant at p < .05. Since our results (3.562) are well below that number, they are not valid at p < .05; in fact, the table indicates that the results are not even valid at p < .30, so we cannot reject H_0.

We can take a further example from Labov 1966:81, the department store survey, to illustrate further the use of X^2. The numbers here refer to subjects who had all, some, or no postvocalic /r/ constriction in their responses to Labov's questionnaire. All the subjects were from Saks Fifth Avenue, and were divided in terms of whether they worked on the lower floors or on the more prestigious upper ones. The null hypothesis, of course, is that there is no relationship between postvocalic /r/ constriction and the prestige of the floor on which the employees worked:

	Ground Floor	Upper Floors	Total	%
All /r/	7	13	20	29.4
Some /r/	7	15	22	32.4

44

No /r/	16	10	26	38.2
Total	30	38	68	100.0

As before, we first calculate the expected scores for each column, and list these in parentheses:

	Ground Floor	Upper Floors
All /r/	7 (8.82)	13 (11.18)
Some /r/	7 (9.71)	15 (12.29)
No /r/	16 (11.47)	10 (14.53)

Now we apply the formula:

$$X^2 = \frac{(7 - 8.82)^2}{8.82} + \frac{(7 - 9.71)^2}{9.71} + \frac{(16 - 11.47)^2}{11.47}$$

$$+ \frac{13 - 11.18)^2}{11.18} + \frac{(15 - 12.29)^2}{12.29} + \frac{(10 - 14.53)^2}{14.53}$$

$$= 5.23$$

After calculating the degrees of freedom (df = [3 − 1] [2 − 1] = 2), we check Table A-3, and find that our result is significant only at p < .10. It is larger than 4.605, but smaller than 5.991, the critical value for X^2 at p < .02 when df = 2.

Labov 1966:57 says that, given the more prestigious status of the upper floors at Saks, "we should find a differential of [postvocalic /r/ constriction]." Perhaps we *should* have, but there is still a 10% probability that his results are a function of chance alone and are valid only for his samples. Put simply, given the level of significance generally accepted in the social sciences, we should not posit a relationship between the floors on which the employees worked and their levels of postvocalic /r/ constriction.

Several linguists, notably Fasold 1972, Wolfram 1974, and Biondi 1975, use X^2 in what are called 2 by 2 tables. That is, there are 2 rows and 2 columns, so df = (2 − 1) (2 −1) = 1, and the table looks as follows:

a	b
c	d

The X^2 calculation is much less time-consuming for such tables:

$$X^2 = \frac{n\ (ad - bc)^2}{(a + c)\ (a + b)\ (b + d)\ (c + d)}$$

The "n" is the total number of observations, and we put in the numbers for each cell, according to the above formula.

Some statisticians recommend using the *Yates Correction for Continuity*, which involves adding 1 additional element to the above formula: subtracting one half of the total n from the difference between ad and bc in the table:

$$X^2 = \frac{n\ \left([ad - bc] - \frac{n}{2}\right)^2}{(a + c)\ (a + b)\ (b + d)\ (c + d)}$$

Although statisticians such as Connover 1974 have objected to the use of the Yates Correction, we linguists would be wise to employ it. It will help prevent us from rejecting H_o by mistake (known as a Type I error).

Note now the following data—the results of Labov's subjective reaction test for postvocalic /r/ constriction:

From /r/– Pronouncing Region	From/r/-less Region	Total

/r/ Positive	10	5	15
/r/ Negative	7	10	17
Total	17	15	32

Using the Yates Correction, we calculate X^2 in the following way:

$$X^2 = \frac{n \left([ad - bc] - \frac{n}{2}\right)^2}{(a + c)(a + b)(b + d)(c + d)}$$

$$= \frac{32 \left([(10 \times 10) - \langle 7 \times 5 \rangle] - \frac{32}{2}\right)^2}{17 \times 15 \times 15 \times 17}$$

$$= \frac{32 \times 49^2}{65,025} = \frac{76,832}{65,025} = 1.18$$

We noted earlier that df $= (2 - 1)(2 - 1) = 1$, and Table A-3 indicates that the results are valid only at $p < .30$. The calculated X^2 (1.18) is larger than 1.074 (X^2 at $p < .30$, where df $= 1$). We cannot, therefore, reject H_o. Given the $p < .05$ level of confidence, we must admit that there is no statistically significant relationship in Labov's population between the response to postvocalic /r/ constriction and the dialect areas from which the people came.

Here a few words of caution are in order insofar as the use of X^2 is concerned. Cochran 1954 demonstrated that, for the test to be valid, no expected frequency can be less than 1, and no more than 20% of all the expected frequencies can be less than 5. For 2 x 2 tables, all of the expected frequencies must be 5 or more. In addition, the proportion test is always a good alternative to X^2, when 2 x 2 tables are involved. Furthermore, X^2 must be used on the actual observed frequencies. **The test cannot be performed on percentages.** When one must deal with percentages, (s)he must either convert them to actual frequencies or use the proportion test.

Up to now, we have been using X^2 to test numbers of subjects. When we are concerned with individual responses, however, we should always set up a frequency distribution. The reason for this involves the fact that the X^2 test requires grouping all the observed frequencies into categories, and this may suggest more homogeneity in the data than the data themselves warrant.

To illustrate this point, we can turn to Feagin's 1979 study of Anniston, Alabama. She presents the results for multiple negation for the older men and women of the rural working class, where the women in her sample, she says, used multiple negation 75.7% of the time and the men used it 88.9% of the time. According to Feagin $X^2 = 9.00$, so the results are supposedly valid at p < .01:

Multiple negation	Men	Women	Total
Yes	129	128	257
No	16	41	57

We can now calculate X^2 using the Yates Correction:

$$X^2 = \frac{314 \left\{ [(129 \times 41) - (128 \times 16)] - \frac{314}{2} \right\}^2}{145 \times 257 \times 169 \times 57}$$

$$= 8.32$$

If we had not used Yates, our results would have been 9.19, or slightly higher than the 9.0 mentioned by Feagin. At df = 1, Table A-3 indeed indicates that p < .01 for multiple negation between the males and the females, so we surely should be able to reject H_o. Our X^2 test suggests that the men of Anniston use multiple negation more than the women do.

However, we noted earler that, whenever possible, data should be put in a frequency distribution before testing. Since Feagin 1979:359 does present the subject by subject responses in an appendix, it is instructive to examine the results in more detail:

RURAL WORKING CLASS

	Men			Women	
Subject	Types/Tokens	%	Subject	Types/Tokens	%
1	55/65	84.62	8	59/66	89.39
2	30/33	90.91	9	24/31	77.42
3	12/12	100.00	10	14/16	87.50
4	5/5	100.00	11	7/13	53.85
5	11/12	91.67	12	4/4	100.00
6	11/12	91.67	13	2/6	12.50
7	5/6	83.33	14	10/11	90.91
			15	8/12	66.67
Totals	129/145	88.97		128/169	75.73

Feagin's means, then, are a function of the **total** cases of multiple negation for the men and women. If we calculate the means for the frequency distributions, however, we obtain different results: 91.74 ($s = 6.56$) for the men and 72.28 ($s = 28.31$) for the women—a difference of nearly 20%.

We should also note that subjects 8 and 9 produced well over half of the potential and actual multiple negations of the women, and likewise for subjects 1 and 2 for the men. The data are hardly homogeneous. Because the F-test shows wide differences between the variances of the two samples, and since the number of subjects in each group is not equal, we probably should not perform the t-test. In this case,

49

however, the Mann-Whitney test (see pp. 37-39) is indeed appropriate:

Men		Women		Rank of Men	Rank of Women
1.	84. 62	8.	89.39	6	8
2.	90.91	9.	77.42	9.5	4
3.	100.00	10.	87.50	14	7
4.	100.00	11.	53.85	14	2
5.	91.67	12.	100.00	11.5	14
6.	91.67	13.	12.50	11.5	1
7.	83.33	14.	90.91	5	9.5
		15.	66.67		3

$$n_1 = 7 \quad n_2 = 8 \quad R_1 = 71.5 \quad R_2 = 48.5$$

$$U = n_1 \, n_2 + \frac{n_1 \, (n_1 + 1)}{2} - R_1$$

$$= (7 \times 8) + \frac{7 \, (7 + 1)}{2} - 71.5$$

$$= 56 + 32 - 71.5 = 16.5$$

If we calculate z, we obtain the following:

$$z = \frac{U - \dfrac{n_1 \, n_2}{2}}{\sqrt{\dfrac{n_1 \, n_2 \, (n_1 + n_2 + 1)}{12}}}$$

$$= \frac{16.5 - 28}{\sqrt{\dfrac{56 \, (7 + 8 + 1)}{12}}} = \frac{-11.5}{8.64} = -1.331$$

Therefore: $p > .05$

The Mann-Whitney test, as we see, reveals that Feagin's results do not justify rejecting H_O at $p < .05$, even though the X^2 test was valid at an even higher level of confidence ($p < .01$). Such is the danger of grouping frequencies together.

One could well argue that the Mann-Whitney test might not be appropriate here because, as we saw, 2 male and 2 female subjects contributed disproportionately to the totals of their respective groups. This is true, but it is even more a problem regarding Feagin's use of X^2. The Mann-Whitney test at least does not force us to group the responses of all the men and all the women together; indeed, we have more control over the data with the Mann–Whitney test than with X^2.

As noted above, X^2 is a very useful test when we are counting subjects rather than actual vs. potential frequencies. In the latter case, we should always set up a frequency distribution. When parametric tests (the t-test, for example) are possible, we should use them; if not, then an equivalent nonparametric test is the appropriate substitute.

4.5 The Coefficient of Correlation

During the discussion of frequency distributions in Chapter 3, we noted that even perfectly reasonable and rational divisions of subjects into classes can lead to misinterpretations of data. We then noted that we could use the coefficient of correlation (r) rather than other methods, because r provides an excellent method for determining the exact relationship between 2 continuous variables; that is, how closely the relationship between two continuous variables is linear and approaches a straight line. Take, for example, the pairs 3 and 4, 4 and 5, and 5 and 6. Were we to graph them, they would form a straight line; and the second number is totally a function of and predictable by the first. In Figure 4-1, taken from Davis and Houck 1989, each small circle represents one pair of data—a southern pronunciation ("Southern Form") and how far south the subject's community lies ("Distance South"):

Figure 4-1. Regression Line

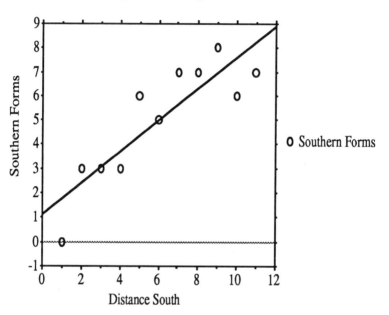

We can see here that the dots do indeed cluster about the line. How the line is drawn is a function of *regression analysis*, which is outside the realm of this book, but the clustering itself provides pictorial evidence for a strong correlation between whatever the two variables happen to be.

The formula for the coefficient of correlation is as follows:

$$r = \frac{n\Sigma xy - [(\Sigma x)\,(\Sigma y)]}{\sqrt{\left[n\Sigma x^2 - (\Sigma x)^2\right]\left[n\Sigma y^2 - (\Sigma y)^2\right]}}$$

Let us now return to Table 3-4, discussed in the section on the frequency distribution. For convenience, the data have been reproduced below in Table 4-2. For our purposes, x = socioeconomic rank score and y = the percent [?] realization of /t/. $\sum x^2$ and $\sum y^2$ equal the sums of the squares of each of the scores, respectively. $(\sum x)^2$ and $(\sum y)^2$ equal the square of the added x and y scores. The calculation is as follows:

Table 4-2. Calculation of r

Subject	x	y	x^2	y^2	xy
1.	30	15	900	225	450
2.	37	25	1,369	625	925
3.	57	20	3,249	400	1,140
4.	61	10	3,721	100	610
5.	69	70	4,761	4,900	4,830
6.	72	35	5,184	1,225	2,520
7.	91	20	8,281	400	1,820
8.	103	40	10,609	1,600	4,120
9.	123	100	15,129	10,000	12,300
10.	125	80	15,625	6,400	10,000
11.	127	20	16,129	400	2,540
12.	130	10	16,900	100	1,300
13.	131	15	17,161	225	1,965
14.	132	60	17,424	3,600	7,920
15.	156	80	24,336	6,400	12,480
16.	156	65	24,336	4,225	10,140
17.	167	65	27,889	4,225	10,855
18.	168	60	28,224	3,600	10,080
19.	185	10	34,225	100	1,850
20.	205	85	42,025	7,225	17,425

$$\sum x = 2,325 \qquad \sum y = 885$$

$$\Sigma x^2 = 317,477 \qquad \Sigma y^2 = 55,975$$

$$\Sigma xy = 115,270$$

$$(\Sigma x)^2 = 5,405,625 \quad (\Sigma y)^2 = 783,225$$

Now we put these values into the formula for the coefficient of correlation:

$$r = \frac{(20 \times 115,270) - (2,325 \times 885)}{\sqrt{[(20 \times 317,477) - 5,405,625]\,[(20 \times 55,975) - 783,225]}}$$

$$= \frac{2,305,400 - 2,057,625}{\sqrt{943,915 \times 336,275}}$$

$$= \frac{247,775}{563,395.9679} = 0.4398$$

Once r is calculated, we can test the null hypothesis by using the following formula, where df $= n - 2$:

$$t = r \sqrt{\frac{n-2}{1-r^2}}$$

$$= .4398 \times \sqrt{\frac{18}{1 - .1934^2}} = 2.0776$$

In Table A-1, the symbol ∞ indicates all degrees of freedom over 30.[3] Since $t_{.05} = 1.960$, we can reject H_0 and say that a relationship does exist between social class rank and [?] realization of /t/.

In addition to providing a useful test for the relationship between a particular variable and social class, r can also be used to show the relationship between 2 linguistic variables. Table 4–3 comes from Anshen 1978:29, and gives the subjects' percentages for [n] realization of /ŋ/ in present participles and [d] realization of /ð/.

Table 4-3. [n] Realization of /ŋ/ and [d] Realization of /ð/

Subject	[ŋ]	[d]
1.	0.0	79.0
2.	11.7	100.0
3.	30.8	58.7
4.	8.3	33.0
5.	0.0	76.3
6.	13.3	45.0
7.	0.0	86.1
8.	13.3	48.4
9.	20.0	22.9
10.	0.0	66.7
11.	0.0	59.3
12.	0.0	89.3
13.	0.0	92.5
14.	100.0	24.0
15.	0.0	66.7
16.	100.0	90.5
17.	64.3	64.6
18.	0.0	45.8
19.	7.1	23.0
20.	7.1	60.7
21.	66.7	100.0
22.	7.2	41.2
23.	0.0	81.5
24.	42.8	100.0
25.	21.4	70.2
26.	0.0	20.0
27.	20.0	64.8
28.	0.0	27.1

29.	0.0	73.7
30.	80.0	85.1
31.	84.6	68.1
32.	66.7	79.9
33.	21.4	85.2
34.	0.0	40.0
35.	10.0	4.0
36.	0.0	73.3
37.	6.7	81.8
38.	71.4	98.0
39.	30.8	51.4
40.	0.0	91.7
41.	78.6	69.2
42.	16.7	54.6
43.	63.3	66.7
44.	22.8	35.7
45.	16.7	50.0
46.	0.0	6.7
47.	0.0	0.0
48.	0.0	0.0
49.	0.0	0.0
50.	0.0	0.0
51.	30.0	46.6
52.	7.1	0.0
53.	0.0	0.0
54.	32.1	86.8
55.	15.4	15.4
56.	0.0	0.0
57.	0.0	0.0
58.	0.0	0.0
59.	0.0	0.0
60.	0.0	0.0
61.	53.3	92.9
62.	0.0	0.0
63.	16.6	25.0
64.	83.3	93.3

65.	71.4	92.9
66.	23.3	66.7
67.	36.7	42.8
68.	10.7	20.0
69.	27.6	60.0

Now we can ask if there is a correlation between the use of [n] in present participles and the use of [d] for /ð/. That is, can we say that the same people who pronounce /ŋ/ as [n] also tend to pronounce /ð/ as [d]? The data for the formula are presented below (n = 69):

$$\Sigma x = 3494.8 \qquad \Sigma y = 1511.8$$
$$\Sigma x^2 = 253{,}841.1 \qquad \Sigma y^2 = 89{,}398.2$$
$$\Sigma xy = 105{,}531.56$$
$$(\Sigma x)^2 = 12{,}213{,}627.04 \qquad (\Sigma y)^2 = 2{,}285{,}539.24$$

We put these numbers in the formula for the coefficient of correlation:

$$r = \frac{n\Sigma xy - [(\Sigma x)\,(\Sigma y)]}{\sqrt{[n\Sigma x^2 - (\Sigma x)^2]\,[n\Sigma y^2 - (\Sigma y)^2]}}$$

$$= \frac{1{,}992{,}194.56}{4{,}537{,}072.989} = 0.4391$$

To test the null hypothesis, we must solve for t:

$$t = .4391 \times \sqrt{\frac{67}{1 - .4391^2}} = 4.005$$

Since df = 67 (n − 2 = 67), greater than 30, and since our calculated t is larger than 3.297, the relationship between the two variables [n] and [d] exists at p < .001—a strong relationship indeed.

Sometimes the calculated value for *r* is a negative number. In earlier cases, we noted that one can ignore the minus sign (for the *t*-test, for example). The minus sign for the correlation coefficient, on the other hand, is extremely important, since it indicates a negative, or inverse correlation: the larger one variable in a pair is, the smaller the second member will be.

The following shows the calculations of *r* for the data in Table 3-1, reproduced for convenience as Table 4-4:

Table 4-4. A-Prefixing in Southern Appalachia

Females % a-prefixing

Subject	Age	%
1	34	47
2	31	32
3	42	16
4	30	25
6	31	68
7	40	14
8	38	56
9	29	25
10	27	70

Males % a-prefixing

Subject	Age	%
11	42	49
12	28	73
13	43	29
14	32	57
15	31	67
16	27	93
17	36	18

$$
\begin{array}{ccc}
18 & 40 & 25 \\
19 & 33 & 76 \\
20 & 29 & 83
\end{array}
$$

$$\Sigma x = 675 \qquad \Sigma y = 970$$

$$\Sigma x^2 = 23{,}317 \qquad \Sigma y^2 = 58{,}376$$

$$\Sigma xy = 31{,}251$$

$$(\Sigma x)^2 = 455{,}625 \qquad (\Sigma y)^2 = 940{,}990$$

$$r = \frac{(20 \times 31{,}251) - (675 \times 970)}{\sqrt{[(20 \times 23{,}317) - 455{,}625][(20 \times 58{,}376) - 940{,}990]}}$$

$$= -.6033$$

$$t = -.6033 \times \sqrt{\frac{8}{1 - (-.60331)^2}} = -3.2095$$

Since t is an absolute value, we can ignore the minus sign for a moment. Table A-1 tells us that at df = 18 we can reject H_0 at $p < .005$ ($t_{005} = 3.197$, and $t_{0025} = 3.610$, and our result falls between these two scores).

The coefficient of correlation for the data on age versus a-prefixing is –0.6033, significant at $p < .01$. The minus sign for r is important, because it means that we have an inverse correlation: the older the subjects are, the less they exhibit a-prefixing.

Further analysis of these data, however, reveals that they are not particularly homogeneous. That is, the r for the females (–0.4687) does not allow us to reject H_0 at $p < .05$ ($t = 1.5007$), whereas the r for the males (–0.8120) is quite high, showing an inverse correlation significant at $p < .005$. You might want to go through these calculations yourself, but the fact is that the lack of homogeneity in the data means that the high r for the males influenced the frequency distribution as a whole, and gave us preliminary results that could be rather misleading. There is a high inverse correlation only insofar as the males are concerned. Moreover, when we calculated the t-test on the means of the females and the males (pp. 30-31), we found that we could not reject H_O at $p < .05$.

4.6 Spearman's *Rho*

Sometimes, the data for two variables are not continuous, so we have to use the nonparametric test proposed by Spearman 1904. This test requires ranking the 2 variables measured, and can be illustrated using the first 10 subjects in Table 3-4. The first column lists the subjects; the second the score the subjects received for socioeconomic class; the third column (%) indicates the percent glottal stop realization of /t/; the next two columns contain the ranks of the socioeconomic class scores (x) and the ranks of the percent glottal stop realization of /t/ (y); the last two columns are social class rank minus glottal stop realization rank (x − y) and the square of this difference $(x - y)^2$:

			Ranks			
Subject	Score	%	x	y	$(x - y)$	$(x - y)^2$
1	30	15	1	2	−1	1
2	37	25	2	5	−3	9
3	57	20	3	3.5	−0.5	0.25
4	61	10	4	1	3	9
5	69	70	5	8	−3	9
6	72	35	6	6	0	0
7	91	20	7	3.5	3.5	12.5
8	103	40	8	7	1	1
9	123	100	9	10	−1	1
10	125	80	10	9	1	1

$$\Sigma(x - y)^2 = 43.50$$

Spearman's *Rho* (r_S), as it is called, requires the following formula:

$$r_S = 1 - \frac{6 \sum (x - y)^2}{n(n^2 - 1)}$$

Since $(x - y)^2$ is 43.50, we can calculate r_S:

$$r_S = 1 - \frac{6 \times 43.50}{10(10^2 - 1)}$$

$$= 1 - \frac{261}{990} = .7364$$

Generally, one needs a special table (not presented here) to evaluate r_S. Chau 1974:459 suggests, however, that we can convert r_S to t in the same way we did for the parametric coefficient of correlation (r). If we do this with the formula on page 53, we obtain the following results, with df $= n - 2 = 10 - 2 = 8$:

$$t = .7364 \times \sqrt{\frac{8}{1 - .7364^2}} = 3.0787$$

According to Table A-1, $t_{.025} = 2.896$ at df $= 8$, so the results here are significant at $p < .025$. If we calculate r, we get $r = .7414$, also significant at $p < .025$. For these results, then, the parametric and nonparametric tests give the same result; however, this is not always the case.

In addition, Spearman's *Rho* is only 90% as powerful as r; that is, r is a better measure of correlation, and we should use it whenever it is appropriate. r_S is 10% more likely to result in our rejecting H_0 by mistake.

One cannot close this section on correlation without expressing a very large caveat: do not assume that a high correlation in any way implies some causality. That is, a high value of one element does not cause a high value of another. Lapin 1975:375 presents the following data from the *Yearbook of Fishery Statistics*, published by the United Nations, and from the *Economic Report of the President*, February 1970:

Year	No. of Sperm Whales Caught	Standard and Poor's Stock Price Index
1964	29,000	81
1965	25,000	88
1966	27,000	85
1967	26,000	92
1968	24,000	99

The calculated r here is -0.886, which indicates an inverse correlation significant at $p < .05$. On the other hand, it would take a great deal of imagination and intellectual gymnastics to determine how the stock market inversely influences, or is inversely influenced by, the number of whales killed in this 5–year period. The correlation exists, but to posit causality is to misunderstand totally the nature of the coefficient of correlation.

4.7   Analysis of Variance

Sometimes we need to compare more than 2 means, and, to do so, we use the square of the standard deviation, s^2--the variance. Hence, the test itself is called analysis of variance. The following data, from Macaulay 1977:174, involve 4 speakers and the linguistic environments in which they use glottal stop:

Speaker	% [?] / ___C	% [?] / ___V	% [?] / ___#
1	69.4	37.5	0

2	52.3	3.3	16.7
3	8.4	27.8	8.3
4	52.5	2.8	0

$$m_1 = 45.65 \qquad m_2 = 17.8 \qquad m_3 = 6.25$$
$$s_1 = 23.78 \qquad s_2 = 17.5 \qquad s_3 = 8.0$$
$$s_1^2 = 565.42 \qquad s_2^2 = 306.2 \qquad s_3^2 = 64.00$$

To analyze these findings, we must first calculate $\hat{s}^2$, which is the variance within the sample:

$$\hat{s}^2 = \frac{s_1^2 + s_2^2 + s_3^2}{\text{Number of Columns}} = \frac{565.42 + 306.2 + 64}{3} = 146.93$$

The mean of three means (m) here is:

$$m = \frac{45.65 + 17.8 + 6.25}{3} = 23.23$$

To calculate the variance between samples $\left(S_m^2\right)$, we multiply the number of horizontal rows (4) times the square of the sum of the differences between each mean and m, and divide by the number of columns minus 1 (c - 1):

$$S_m^2 = \frac{4\left[(m_1 - m)^2 + (m_2 - m)^2 + (m_3 - m)^2\right]}{c - 1}$$

$$= \frac{4\left[(45.65 - 23.23)^2 + (17.8 - 23.23)^2 + (6.25 - 23.23)^2)\right]}{2}$$

$$= 1,640.92$$

To see if the difference between the above means is significant, we divide the variance between samples $\left(S_m^2\right)$ by the variance within samples $\left(\widehat{S}^2\right)$:

$$F = \frac{S_m^2}{\widehat{S}^2} = \frac{1,640.92}{311.87} = 5.26$$

Now we turn to Table A-2, the F-Distribution. Degrees of freedom are calculated as follows:

$$
\begin{aligned}
\text{Vertical df} &= c - 1 \\
&= 3 - 1 = 2 \\
\text{Horizontal df} &= c\,(r - 1) \\
&= 3\,(4 - 1) = 9
\end{aligned}
$$

Table A-2, at $F_{.05\,(2,\,9)}$, reveals that we need a value of at least 4.26 to reject H_0 at $p < .05$ and 8.02 to reject H_0 at $p < .01$, so our results (5.26) are significant at $p < .05$.

Another way of calculating the variance between columns is far more laborious than simply calculating, as we did above, the mean of the variances. This alternative method involves calculating the sum of the squares of the differences between each finding in the above table and the mean for the respective columns: $(69.4 - 45.65)^2 + (52.3 - 45.65)^2 + (37.5 - 17.8)^2$ and so on. This number is then divided by the number of horizontal degrees of freedom (9). Since it is indeed far more cumbersome, and leads essentially to the same results, this method is recommended exclusively for those readers who enjoy using their calculators.

As with the *t*-test, the analysis of variance requires that the data be continuous and that the populations from which the samples were taken have essentially equal variances. Bartlett 1937 provided a test for population variances. More recently, statisticians such as Box and Anderson 1955 and

Tiku 1971 have argued that analysis of variance is a good test even when there are wide differences between the sample (therefore population) variances. In any case, the data must be continuous.

In the case just discussed, where [?] was analyzed in 3 different linguistic environments, the data are continuous, but we have an extremely wide gap between the variances of columns 2 (306.2) and 3 (64). This large difference in variances suggests that we turn to a nonparametric test, called the Kruskall-Wallis test, that makes no assumptions about the population variances involved (Kruskall and Wallis 1952).

The test itself involves ranking each score respective to all the others. Ties are handled in the same way as with the Mann-Whitney test (see pp. 37-39).

The following is the table we used above for glottal stop. The ranks of the scores are listed in parentheses. The sums of the ranks for each column are listed also as R_1, R_2, and R_3, respectively:

Speaker	% [?] / ___C	% [?] / ___V	% [?] / ___#
1	69.4 (12)	37.5 (9)	0 (1.5)
2	52.3 (10)	3.3 (4)	16.7 (7)
3	8.4 (6)	27.8 (8)	8.3 (5)
4	52.5 (11)	2.8 (3)	0 (1.5)
	$R_1 = 42$	$R_2 = 22$	$R_3 = 14$
	$n_1 = 4$	$n_2 = 4$	$n_3 = 4$
		$N = 12$	

We now calculate the Kruskall-Wallis statistic, H:

$$H = \frac{12}{N(N+1)} \sum \frac{R_i^2}{n_i} - 3(N+1)$$

$$= \frac{12}{12\,(12+1)} \left[\frac{39^2}{4} + \frac{24^2}{4} + \frac{15^2}{4} \right] - 3\,(12+1)$$

$$= \left(\frac{12}{156} \times 580.5 \right) - 39$$

$$= 44.64 - 39 = 5.64$$

Although a special table does exist for H, we may also use the X^2 table and calculate df as $(c-1) = 3-1 = 2$. At df $= 2$, we see that $X^2_{.05} = 5.991$. In other words, the Kruskall–Wallis test does not allow us to reject H_O at $p < .05$; thus it gives a different result from the parametric analysis of variance. Contradictions of this kind seldom occur. When they do, the best course of action is to state one's conclusions quite tentatively and, without a doubt, seek the advice of a good applied statistician. In the above case, we probably should not reject H_O. The variances are simply too different between columns 2 and 3.

To take another example, suppose that a linguistic survey in Indiana studied 15 subjects—5 from each of 3 different locations—with respect to multiple negation. The following results were obtained in percentages:

	Place	
I	II	III
56	48	55
60	61	50
50	48	42
65	52	33
64	46	40

$$m_1 = 59 \quad m_2 = 51 \quad m_3 = 44$$

$$s_1^2 = 38.4 \quad s_2^2 = 36.0 \quad s_3^2 = 74.0$$

$$m = \frac{59 + 51 + 44}{3} = 51.3$$

$$S_m^2 = \frac{5\left[(59 - 51.3)^2 + (51 - 51.3)^2 + (44 - 51.3)^2\right]}{3 - 1}$$

$$= 281.65$$

$$\widehat{S}^2 = \frac{38.4 + 36 + 74}{3} = 49.5$$

$$F = \frac{281.65}{49.5} = 5.6899$$

vertical df $= 3 - 1 = 2$
horizontal df $= 3 (5 - 1) = 12$

$F_{.05\ (2,12)} = 3.88 \quad F_{.01\ (2,12)} = 6.93$

Therefore: We can reject H_o at $p < .05$, but not at $p < .01$.

The results for the Kruskall-Wallis test on these same data are presented below. $R_1 = 59.5$, $R_2 = 37.0$, and $R_3 = 23.5$:

$$H = \frac{12}{15 \times 16} \left[\frac{59.5^2}{5} + \frac{37^2}{5} + \frac{23.5^2}{5} \right] - 3 (15 + 1)$$

$$= 6.615$$

According to the X^2 table at df $= 2$, our results are significant at $p < .05$ ($X^2 = 5.991$), but not at $p < .02$ ($X^2 = 7.824$); that is, both the parametric analysis of variance and the Kruskall-Wallis test gave us the same results.

A general rule for analysis of variance is that whenever the linguist has reason to suspect that population variances are not equal, (s)he should double-check the parametric test with Kruskall-Wallis. Always reject H_0 at the lower confidence level. As noted earlier, if the parametric analysis of variance and the Kruskall-Wallis test disagree as to the rejection or acceptance of the null hypothesis, one would do well to consult a statistician. Decision rules in such cases are sometimes quite specific to the data involved, and are out of the range of this book.

4.8   2-Way Analysis of Variance

Table 4-5. Mean Scores for Pleasantness of Voice
2 Male and 2 Female Speakers as Judged by
4 Groups of Subjects in 4 Cities

| | Atlanta | | Boston | | |
	Male	Female	Male	Female	Sample Mean
London	65	74	70	71	$sm_1 = 70.0$
Chicago	85	82	85	80	$sm_2 = 83.0$
New York	88	91	80	85	$sm_3 = 86.0$
Sheffield	84	89	69	82	$sm_4 = 81.0$

$mc_1 = 80.5$ $mc_2 = 84$ $mc_3 = 79$ $mc_4 = 79.5$ $m = 80.0$

The data in Table 4-5 permit us to ask 2 different questions: (1) Is there a relationship between how the male speakers are judged, as opposed to the females? (2) Is the city in which the subjects live relevant to their judgments as to the pleasantness of the voices of the speakers? To answer these questions together, we can use 2-way analysis of variance, and the test itself makes the same assumption about population variances as have the other parametric tests discussed here.

The $m = 80$ in the lower right corner of Table 4-5 is the mean of the sample means (sm). First, we calculate the sum of the squares (SS) of the differences between m and each

68

response in the table:

Total SS =
$(65 - 80)^2 = 225$ $(74 - 80)^2 = 36$ $(70 - 80)^2 = 100$
$(71 - 80)^2 = 81$ $(85 - 80)^2 = 25$ $(82 - 80)^2 = 4$
$(85 - 80)^2 = 25$ $(80 - 80)^2 = 0$ $(88 - 80)^2 = 64$
$(91 - 80)^2 = 121$ $(80 - 80)^2 = 0$ $(85 - 80)^2 = 25$
$(84 - 80)^2 = 16$ $(89 - 80)^2 = 81$ $(69 - 80)^2 = 121$
$(82 - 80)^2 = 4$
Total SS = 928

Our next calculation is to multiply the number of rows (4) by the sum of the squares of the differences between m and the means of each column (mc $- m$), as we did for one-way analysis of variance. We will call this result SSA, between columns variation:

$$SSA = r [\Sigma (mc - m)^2]$$
$$= 4 [(80.5 - 80)^2 + (84 - 80)^2 + (76 - 80)^2 + (79.5 - 80)^2]$$
$$= 130$$

Now, we do the same thing to calculate SSB, the variation between the rows. Here, we multiply the number of columns times the squares of the differences between m and the means for the 4 rows:

$$SSB = c [\Sigma (mr - m)^2]$$
$$= 4 [(70 - 80)^2 + (83 - 80)^2 + (86 - 80)^2 + (81 - 80)^2]$$
$$= 584$$

The difference between the total sum of squares (SS = 928) and SSA and SSB is calculated as follows:

$$SD = SS - SSA - SSB$$

$$= 928 - 130 - 584$$
$$= 214$$

To find factor A, if the sex of the speakers influence how they were judged, we must calculate F, as we did for one-way analysis of variance. Here, however, the formula is different:

$$F = \frac{MSA}{MSD}$$

Where $MSA = \dfrac{SSA}{c-1} = \dfrac{130}{4-1} = 43.33$

and $MSD = \dfrac{SD}{(r-1)\,(c-1)} = \dfrac{214}{9} = 23.78$

Now we can calculate F for factor A:

$$F = \frac{43.33}{23.78} = 1.8221$$

For factor B, whether the cities from which the judges came influenced their responses, we perform the analogous tests to those for factor A:

$$F = \frac{MSB}{MSD}$$

Where $MSB = \dfrac{SSB}{c-1} = \dfrac{584}{4-1} = 194.67$

and MSD (calculated above) $= 23.78$

We calculate F for factor B by dividing MSB by MSD:

$$F = \frac{194.67}{23.78} = 8.1863$$

Before going to the F-Table (Table A-2), we must first calculate the vertical and horizontal degrees of freedom (respectively, the numerator and the denominator):

For A (between columns):

$$\text{Vertical df} = c - 1 = 4 - 1 = 3$$
$$\text{Horizontal df} = r\,(r - 1) = 4\,(4 - 1) = 12$$

For B (between rows):

$$\text{Vertical df} = r - 1 = 4 - 1 = 3$$
$$\text{Horizontal df} = r\,(c - 1) = 4\,(4 - 1) = 12$$

Since $F_{.05\ (3,\ 12)} = 3.49$, our results for factor A (1.8221) do not permit us to reject H_O at $p < .05$, so we can say that there appears to be no relationship between the sex of the speakers and the subjects' judgments regarding the pleasantness of the speakers' voices.

On the other hand, the results for factor B (8.1863) allow us to reject H_O at a level of confidence of $p < .01$. That is, a relationship does exist between the cities in which the subjects live and the way they judged the speakers' voices.

4.9   Conclusion

The statistical tests discussed in this book and the criteria for their application can be summarized in the following outline:

I. Frequency distributions
    A. Comparison of 2 means
        1. Parametric conditions: (1) continuous data and (2)

the F-test
    a. Large sample test (n > 30)
    b. t-test (n ≤ 30)
2. Nonparametric test: Mann-Whitney
B. Comparison of 3 or more means
    1. Parametric conditions: (1) continuous data and (2) small differences among the variances of the samples.
       a. Analysis of variance
       b. 2-way analysis of variance
    2. Nonparamentric test: Kruskall-Wallis
C. Correlation
    1. Parametric condition: continuous data
    2. Nonparametric test: Spearman's *Rho*
II. Comparison of Groups of Subjects
    1. Proportion test for percentages
    2. X^2 test
       a. Regular X^2 test where df > 1
       b. X^2 test with the Yates Correction when df = 1

We have now surveyed the major statistical tests that can be used to evaluate linguistic data. All the tests outlined here, but especially the parametric ones, require that certain conditions be met. Without such conditions, one cannot use certain tests with the assurance that H_O will be properly rejected. If, for example, the t-test is performed on samples with widely divergent population variances, it might turn out that the results are deceiving, and that H_O is rejected without due cause. This mistake (known as a Type I error) can be avoided by checking suspicious results with an appropriate nonparametric test.

The most important point made throughout this work is that one cannot allow numbers and tables to speak for themselves. It is not enough to say that one group of people uses a certain form more than another group does; the numbers require statistical interpretation. In addition, the rigor of statistical analysis forces us to live in the world of probabilities rather than certainties. The rejection of the null hypothesis means that we are willing to accept a small degree of uncertainty about our results, so we can never be absolutely confident about our results. We can paraphrase Joos 1966:96 and note that children want certainty, and there is some child in each of us. The use of statistics in dialectology should help make a virtue out of not pampering that child.

Notes

1. There are 2 possible ways to test the null hypothesis. In the last example from Wald and Shopen, H_O could have been simply that the men do not exhibit more (ING) than the women. That is, we could reject H_O if $m_1 > m_2$. The alternative is to define H_O as saying that the means are equal ($m_1 = m_2$), then reject H_O if either mean is significantly ($p < .05$) larger. This latter option, called a *two–tailed test,* is the one utilized here. That is, all the tests in this book are two–tailed wherever possible.

2. Zar 1974:112 points out that the approximation of z here is for levels of significance of $p < .01$ or lower. Strictly speaking, the formula for z is also different when ties are involved. Zar 1974:113 notes that the main denominator for the equation for z should, in fact, be as follows:

$$\sqrt{\frac{n_1\, n_2}{(n_1 + n_2)^2 - (n_1 + n_2)} \times \frac{(n_1 + n_2)^3 - (n_1 + n_2) - T}{12}}$$

Where $T = \sum (t_i^2 - t_i)$, and where t_i is "the number of ties in a group of tied values, and the summation is performed over all groups of ties." Results here and elsewhere in this book are not affected by using the simpler formula.

3. Generally, t-distribution tables list more degrees of freedom than Table A-1. Tables A-1, A-2, and A-3 are provided for illustrative purposes only, so, for serious statistical work, one should consult books of mathematical tables, such as Fisher and Yates 1963.

APPENDICES[1]

---

[1]Tables A-1, A-2, and A-3 were generated using the *Statistical Applications System*, published by SAS, Inc.

MAJOR STATISTICAL FORMULAS
USED IN THIS TEXT

1. Standard deviation:

$$\sqrt{\frac{\sum (O - m)^2}{n - 1}}$$

2. Differences between means: large samples:

a.

$$s_D = \sqrt{\frac{s_1^2}{n_1} + \frac{s_1^2}{n_2}}$$

b.

$$z = \frac{m_1 - m_2}{s_D}$$

3. t-test for differences between means: small samples:

a.

$$s_D = \sqrt{\frac{(n_1 - 1) s_1^2 + (n_1 - 1) s_2^2}{n_1 + n_2 - 2}} \sqrt{\frac{1}{n_1} + \frac{1}{n_2}}$$

b.

$$z = \frac{m_1 - m_2}{s_D}$$

c. $df = m_1 + m_2 - 2$

4. Mann-Whitney test for differences between means:

a.

$$U = n_1 n_2 + \frac{n_1 (n_1 + 1)}{2} - R_1$$

b.

$$z = \frac{U - \frac{n_1 n_2}{2}}{\sqrt{\frac{n_1 n_2 (n_1 + n_2 + 1)}{12}}}$$

5. Proportion test:

a.

$$\pi = \frac{n_1 p_1 + n_2 p_2}{n_1 + n_2}$$

b.

$$z = \frac{p_1 - p_2}{\sqrt{\pi (1 - \pi) \left(\frac{1}{n_1} + \frac{1}{n_2}\right)}}$$

6. Chi square:

a.

$$X^2 = \sum \frac{(actual - expected)^2}{expected}$$

b. $df = (r - 1)(c - 1)$

7. Chi square for 2 by 2 tables ($df = 1$), with the Yates Correction for Continuity:

$$X^2 = \frac{n \left([ad - bc] - \frac{n}{2}\right)^2}{(a + c)(a + b)(b + d)(c + d)}$$

8. Coefficient of correlation:

a.
$$r = \frac{n\Sigma xy - [(\Sigma x)(\Sigma y)]}{\sqrt{[n\Sigma x^2 - (\Sigma x)^2][n\Sigma y^2 - (\Sigma y)^2]}}$$

b.
$$t = r\sqrt{\frac{n-2}{1-r^2}}$$

c. $df = n - 2$

9. Spearman's *Rho*:

a.
$$r_s = 1 - \frac{6\Sigma(x-y)^2}{n(n^2-1)}$$

b.
$$t = r_s\sqrt{\frac{n-2}{1-r_s^2}}$$

c. $df = n - 2$

10. Analysis of variance:

a.
$$\hat{s}^2 = \frac{s_1^2 + s_2^2 + s_3^2}{\text{Number of Columns}}$$

b.
$$m = \frac{\Sigma m_i}{c}$$

c.

$$S_m^2 = \frac{4\left[(m_1 - m)^2 + (m_2 - m)^2 + (m_3 - m)^2\right]}{c - 1}$$

d.

$$F = \frac{S_m^2}{\widehat{S}^2}$$

e. Vertical df $= c - 1$; horizontal df $= c(r - 1)$

11. **Kruskall-Wallis analysis of variance:**

a.

$$H = \frac{12}{N(N+1)} \sum \frac{R_i^2}{n_i} - 3(N+1)$$

b. Use chi square table, where df $= c - 1$

12. 2-way analysis of variance:

a.

$$m = \frac{\sum m_i}{r}$$

b.

$$SSA = r\left[\sum (mc - m)^2\right]$$

c.

$$SSB = c\left[\sum (mr - m)^2\right]$$

d. For factor A:

$$F = \frac{MSA}{MSD}$$

Where MSA $= \dfrac{\text{SSA}}{c-1}$

and MSD $= \dfrac{\text{SD}}{(r-1)\,(c-1)}$

e. For factor B:

$$F = \dfrac{\text{MSB}}{\text{MSD}}$$

Where MSB $= \dfrac{\text{SSB}}{c-1}$

and MSD $= \dfrac{\text{SD}}{(r-1)\,(c-1)}$

f. df for factor A:

Vertical df $= c - 1$
Horizontal df $= r\,(r - 1)$

g. df for factor B:

Vertical df $= r - 1$
Horizontal df $= r\,(c - 1)$

Table A-1. *t*-Distribution

Degrees of Freedom	Levels of Confidence							
	.25	.10	.05	.025	.001	.005	.0025	.001
1	3.078	6.314	12.706	31.821	63.657	127.321	318.309	636.619
2	1.886	2.920	4.303	6.975	9.925	14.089	22.327	31.599
3	1.638	2.353	3.182	4.541	5.841	7.453	10.214	12.924
4	1.533	2.132	2.776	3.747	4.604	5.598	7.713	8.610
5	1.476	2.015	2.571	3.365	4.032	4.773	5.583	6.879
6	1.440	1.993	2.447	3.143	3.707	4.317	5.208	5.959
7	1.415	1.895	2.365	2.998	3.499	4.029	4.785	5.408
8	1.397	1.860	2.306	2.896	3.355	3.833	4.501	5.041
9	1.383	1.833	2.262	2.821	3.250	3.690	4.297	4.781
10	1.372	1.812	2.228	2.764	3.169	3.581	4.144	4.587
11	1.363	1.796	2.201	2.718	3.106	3.497	4.025	4.437
12	1.356	1.782	2.179	2.681	3.055	3.428	3.930	4.318
13	1.350	1.771	2.160	2.650	3.012	3.372	3.852	4.221
14	1.345	1.761	2.145	2.624	2.977	3.326	3.787	4.140
15	1.341	1.753	2.131	2.602	2.947	3.286	3.733	4.073
16	1.337	1.746	2.120	2.583	2.921	3.252	3.686	4.015
17	1.333	1.740	2.110	2.567	2.898	3.222	3.646	3.965
18	1.330	1.734	2.101	2.552	2.878	3.197	3.610	3.922
19	1.328	1.729	2.093	2.539	2.861	3.174	3.579	3.883
20	1.325	1.725	2.086	2.528	2.845	3.153	3.552	3.850
21	1.323	1.721	2.080	2.518	2.831	3.135	3.527	3.819
22	1.321	1.717	2.074	2.518	2.819	3.119	3.505	3.792
23	1.319	1.714	2.069	2.500	2.807	3.104	3.485	3.767
24	1.318	1.711	2.064	2.492	2.797	3.091	3.467	3.745
25	1.316	1.708	2.060	2.485	2.787	3.078	3.450	3.725
26	1.315	1.706	2.056	2.479	2.779	3.067	3.435	3.707
27	1.314	1.703	2.052	2.473	2.771	3.057	3.421	3.690
28	1.313	1.701	2.048	2.467	2.763	3.047	3.408	3.674
29	1.311	1.699	2.045	2.462	2.756	3.038	3.396	3.659
30	1.310	1.697	2.042	2.457	2.750	3.030	3.385	3.646
∞	1.282	1.645	1.960	2.326	2.576	2.807	3.090	3.297

Table A-2. F-Distribution

Vertical Degrees of Freedom	Horizontal Degrees of Freedom					
	1	2	3	4	5	6
2	18.51	19.00	19.16	19.25	19.30	19.33
	98.49	**99.00**	**99.17**	**99.25**	**99.30**	**99.33**
3	10.13	9.55	9.28	9.12	9.01	8.94
	34.12	**30.82**	**29.46**	**28.71**	**28.24**	**27.91**
4	7.71	6.94	6.59	6.39	6.26	6.16
	21.20	**18.00**	**16.69**	**15.98**	**15.52**	**15.21**
5	6.61	5.79	5.41	5.19	5.05	4.95
	16.26	**13.27**	**12.06**	**11.39**	**10.97**	**10.67**
6	5.99	5.14	4.76	4.53	4.39	4.28
	13.64	**10.92**	**9.78**	**9.15**	**8.75**	**8.47**
7	50.59	4.74	4.35	4.12	3.97	3.87
	12.25	**9.55**	**8.45**	**7.85**	**7.46**	**7.19**
8	5.32	4.46	4.07	3.84	3.69	3.58
	11.26	**8.65**	**7.59**	**7.01**	**6.63**	**6.37**
9	5.12	4.26	3.86	3.63	3.48	3.37
	10.56	**8.02**	**6.99**	**6.42**	**6.06**	**5.80**
10	4.96	4.10	3.71	3.48	3.33	3.22
	10.04	**7.56**	**6.55**	**5.99**	**5.64**	**5.39**
11	4.84	3.98	3.59	3.36	3.20	3.09
	9.65	**7.20**	**6.22**	**5.67**	**5.32**	**5.07**
12	4.75	3.88	3.49	3.26	3.11	3.00
	9.33	**6.93**	**5.95**	**5.41**	**5.06**	**4.82**

Table A-2. F-Distribution (continued)

Vertical Degrees of Freedom	Horizontal Degrees of Freedom					
	7	8	9	10	11	12
2	19.36	19.37	19.38	19.39	19.40	19.41
	99.36	**99.37**	**99.39**	**99.40**	**99.41**	**99.42**
3	8.88	8.84	8.81	8.78	8.76	8.74
	27.67	**27.49**	**27.34**	**27.23**	**27.13**	**27.05**
4	6.09	6.04	6.00	5.96	5.93	5.91
	14.98	**14.80**	**14.66**	**14.54**	**14.45**	**14.37**
5	4.88	4.82	4.78	4.74	4.70	4.68
	10.45	**10.29**	**10.15**	**10.05**	**9.96**	**9.89**
6	4.21	4.15	4.10	4.06	4.03	4.00
	8.26	**8.10**	**7.89**	**7.87**	**7.79**	**7.72**
7	3.79	3.73	3.68	3.63	3.60	3.57
	7.00	**6.84**	**6.71**	**6.62**	**6.54**	**6.47**
8	3.50	3.44	3.39	3.34	3.31	3.28
	6.19	**6.03**	**5.91**	**5.82**	**5.74**	**5.67**
9	3.29	3.23	3.18	3.13	3.10	3.07
	5.62	**5.47**	**5.35**	**5.26**	**5.18**	**5.11**
10	3.14	3.07	3.02	2.97	2.94	2.91
	5.21	**5.06**	**4.95**	**4.85**	**4.78**	**4.71**
11	3.01	2.95	2.90	2.86	2.82	2.79
	4.88	**4.74**	**4.63**	**4.54**	**4.46**	**4.40**
12	2.92	2.85	2.80	2.76	2.72	2.69
	4.65	**4.50**	**4.39**	**4.30**	**4.22**	**4.16**

Values for $F_{.05}$ are presented in regular print; those for $F_{.01}$ are in **boldface**.

Table A-3. X^2 Distribution

Degrees of Freedom	Levels of Confidence						
	.30	.20	.10	.05	.02	.01	.001
1	1.074	1.642	2.706	3.841	5.412	6.635	10.827
2	2.408	3.219	4.605	5.991	7.824	9.210	13.815
3	3.665	4.642	6.251	7.815	9.837	11.345	16.268
4	4.878	5.989	7.779	9.488	11.668	13.227	18.465
5	6.064	7.289	9.236	11.070	13.388	15.086	20.517
6	7.231	8.558	10.645	12.592	15.033	16.812	22.457
7	8.383	9.803	12.017	14.067	16.622	18.475	24.322
8	9.524	11.030	13.362	15.507	18.168	20.090	26.125
9	10.656	12.242	14.684	16.919	19.679	21.666	27.877
10	11.781	13.442	15.987	18.307	21.161	23.209	29.588
11	12.899	14.631	17.275	19.675	22.618	24.725	31.264
12	14.011	15.812	18.549	21.026	24.054	26.217	32.909
13	15.119	16.985	19.812	22.362	25.472	27.688	34.528
14	16.222	18.151	21.064	23.685	26.873	29.141	36.123
15	17.322	19.311	22.307	24.996	28.259	30.578	37.697
16	18.418	20.465	23.542	26.296	29.633	32.000	39.252
17	19.511	21.615	24.769	27.587	30.995	33.409	40.790
18	20.601	22.760	25.989	28.869	32.346	34.805	42.312
19	21.689	23.900	27.204	30.144	33.687	36.191	43.820
20	22.775	25.038	28.412	31.410	35.020	37.566	45.315
21	23.858	26.171	29.615	32.671	36.343	38.932	46.797
22	24.939	27.301	30.813	33.924	37.659	40.289	48.268
23	26.018	28.429	32.007	35.172	38.968	41.638	49.728
24	27.096	29.553	33.196	36.415	40.270	42.980	51.179
25	28.172	30.675	34.382	37.652	41.566	44.314	52.620
26	29.246	31.795	35.563	38.885	42.856	45.642	54.052
27	30.319	32.912	36.741	40.113	44.140	46.963	55.476
28	31.391	34.027	37.916	41.337	45.419	48.278	56.893
29	32.461	35.139	39.087	42.551	46.693	49.588	58.302
30	33.530	36.250	40.256	43.773	47.962	50.892	59.703

Works Cited

Anshen, Frank. 1978. *Statistics for Linguists*. Rowley, MA: Newbury House.

Bartlett, M. S. 1937. "Some Examples of Statistical Methods of Research in Agriculture and Applied Biology." *Journal of the Royal Statistical Society Supplement* 4: 137-70.

Baubkus, Lutz, and Wolfgang Viereck. 1973. "Recent American Studies in Sociolinguistics." *Archivum Linguisticum* n. s. 4: 103-11.

Biondi, Lawrence. 1975. *The Italian-American Child: His Sociolinguistic Acculturation*. Washington, DC: Georgetown UP.

Box, G. E. P. 1953. "Non-normality and Tests on Variances." *Biometrika* 40: 318-55.

_____, and S. L. Anderson. 1955. "Permutation Theory in the Derivation of Robust Criteria and the Study of Departures from Assumption." *Journal of the Royal Statistical Society* 17: 1-34.

Butler, Christopher. 1985. *Statistics in Linguistics*. New York: Basil Blackwell.

Cedergren, Henrietta, and David Sankoff. 1974. "Variable Rules: Performance as a Statistical Reflection of Competence." *Language* 50: 333-55.

Chau, Lincoln L. 1974. *Statistics: Methods and Analysis*. New York: McGraw.

Cichocki, Wladyslaw. 1988. "Uses of Dual Scaling in Social Dialectology: Multidimensional Analysis of Vowel Variation." *Methods in Dialectology*. Ed. A. R. Thomas. Clevedon and Philadelphia: Multilingual Matters. 187-99.

Cochran, W. G. 1954. "Some Methods for Strengthening the Common X^2 Tests." *Biometrics* 10: 417-51.

Colton, Theodore. 1974. *Statistics in Medicine*. Boston: Little.

Connover, W. J. 1974. "Some Reasons for Not Using the

Yates Continuity Correction on 2 X 2 Contingency Tables." *Journal of the American Statistical Association* 69: 374-82.

Davis, Lawrence M. 1982. "American Social Dialectology: A Statistical Perspective." *American Speech* 57: 83-94.

_____. 1985. "The Problem of Social Class Grouping in Sociolinguistic Research." *American Speech* 60: 214-221.

_____. 1986. "Sampling and Statistical Inference in Dialectology." *Journal of English Linguistics* 19: 42-48.

_____, and Charles L. Houck. 1989. "Kurath's Midland: Fact or Fiction?" Midwest American Dialect Society, Minneapolis, November.

Dunn, Olive Jean. *Basic Statistics: A Primer for the Biomedical Sciences.* New York: John Wiley and Sons.

Fasold, Ralph W. 1972. *Tense Marking in Black English: A Linguistic and Social Analysis* . Washington, DC: CAL.

Feagin, Crawford. 1979. *Variation and Change in Alabama English: A Sociolinguistic Study of the White Community.* Washington, DC: Georgetown UP.

Fisher, R. A., and F. Yates. 1963. *Statistical Tables for Biological, Agricultural, and Medical Research.* 6th ed. New York: Hafner.

Hatch, Evelyn, and Hossein Farhady. 1982. *Research Design and Statistics for Applied Linguistics.* Rowley, MA: Newbury House.

Houck, Charles L. 1986. "Multi-dimensional Scaling as a Statistical Analytical Procedure." Midwest American Dialect Society, Chicago, November.

Joos, Martin. 1966. *Readings in Linguistics, I.* 4th ed. Chicago: U of Chicago P.

Kruskall, W. H., and W. A. Wallis. 1952. "Use of Ranks in One-Criterion Analysis of Variance." *Journal of the American Statistical Association* 47: 583-621.

86

Kurath, Hans. 1968."The Investigation of Urban Speech." *Publication of the American Dialect Society* 49: 1-7.

Labov, William. 1968. *The Social Stratification of English in New York City*. Washington, DC: CAL.

_____. 1969. "Contraction, Deletion, and Inherent Variability of the English Copula." *Language* 45: 715-62.

Lapin, Lawrence. 1975. *Statistics: Meaning and Method*. New York: Harcourt.

Levine, Lewis, and Harry J. Crockett, Jr. 1966. "Speech Variation in a Piedmont Community: Postvocalic /r/." *Sociological Inquiry* 36.2. Cited from *Explorations in Sociolinguistics*. Ed. S. Lieberman. Part II of *International Journal of American Linguistics* 33.2 (1967): 76-98.

Linn, Michael D. 1983. "Informant Selection in Dialectology." *American Speech* 58: 225-43.

_____, and Ronald R. Regal. 1988. "Verb Analysis of the Linguistic Atlas of the North Central States: A Case Study in Preliminary Analysis of a Large Data Set." *Methods in Dialectology*. Ed. A. R. Thomas. Clevedon and Philadelphia: Multilingual Matters. 138-54.

Macaulay, Ronald K. S. 1977. *Language, Social Class and Education*. Edinburgh: Edinburgh UP.

Milroy, Leslie. 1980. *Language and Social Networks*. Oxford: Basil Blackwell.

Muller, Charles. 1968. *Initiation à la statistique linguistique*. Paris: Larousse.

Pickford, Glenna R. 1956. "American Linguistic Geography: A Sociological Appraisal." *Word* 12: 211-33.

Shuy, Roger W., Walter A. Wolfram, and William K. Riley. 1968. *Field Techniques in an Urban Language Study*. Washington, DC: CAL.

Spearman, Carl. 1904. "The Proof and Measurement of Association Between Two Things." *American Journal of Psychology* 15: 72-101.

Sudman, Seymour. 1976. *Applied Sampling*. New York: Academic Press.

Tiku, A. 1971. "Power Functions of the F-Test Under Normal Situations." *Journal of the American Statistical Association* 66: 913-16.

Trudgill, Peter J. 1974. *The Social Differentiation of English in Norwich*. Cambridge: Cambridge UP.

Wald, Benji, and Timothy Shopen. 1981. "A Researcher's Guide to the Sociolinguistic Variable (ING)." *Style and Variables in English*. Ed. T. Shopen and J. Williams. Cambridge, MA: Winthrop. 219-49.

Wolfram, Walter A. 1969. *A Sociolinguistic Description of Detroit Negro Speech*. Washington, DC: CAL.

____. 1974. *Sociolinguistic Aspects of Assimilation: Puerto Rican English in New York City*. Washington, DC: CAL.

Zar, Jerrold H. 1974. *Biostatistical Analysis*. Englewood Cliffs, NJ: Prentice-Hall.

Index

About the Author

Lawrence M. Davis is Professor of English, Ball State University. He received his B.A. degree from the University of Cincinnati and his Ph.D. degree from the University of Chicago. Among his publications is *English Dialectology: An Introduction* (1983).